Class 50s in Operation

David N. Clough

Ian Allan

PUBLISHING

Contents

Preface   3

Introduction   4

1 English Electric Heritage   6

2 The Class 50 Contract   15

3 The Early Years   23

4 Double-heading and Downgrading   37

5 Transfer to the WR   65

6 Refurbishment   85

7 Run-down to Retirement   95

8 Private Ownership   131

9 The Portuguese 'Class 50s'   139

Appendix   149

Dedication

This book is dedicated to my wife Jo. Since we first met, her interest in – and knowledge of – railways has grown from nil to the point where she is now a proficient railway photographer. This dedication is by way of thanks for the time spent at the lineside and checking printers' proofs.

Front cover: **A fil-in job was the Exeter Riverside—Dover china clay polybulks. On 17 September 1986 No 50017 *RoyalOak* approaches Heywood Road Junction, at the east end of the Westbury loop.** *John Chalcraft*

Back cover: **No D434 makes a fine sight as it negotiates Lancaster Castle station on 31 July 1968 with the down 'Mid-Day Scot'. The water column was still in use at this time.** *David N. Clough*

Back cover centre: **No 50043 *Eagle* departs Cheltenham with the 09.35 Liverpool— Penzance on 14 March 1985.** *John Chalcraft*

Back cover bottom: **The distinctive Railfreight triple grey livery, with Sector decals, was applied to one Class 50, No 50149 *Defiance*. The locomotive is seen on 18 October 1987 on Warminster Bank, Wiltshire, during trials to assess its performance.** *David N. Clough*

Previous page: **No 50003 is seen passing Attercliffe Road, Sheffield, at the head of the 09.50 Edinburgh—Plymouth service on 26 September 1980 following a works visit.** *L. A. Nixon*

Front endpaper: **Nos D430 and D409 passing lamington in the Clyde Valley.** *Derek Cross*

Rear endpaper: **Nos 50031 *Hood* and 50015 *Valiant* at Brent on 21 August 1990.** *C. R. Holland*

First published 2004

ISBN 0 7110 2971 7

Published by Ian Allan Publishing

an imprint of Ian Allan Publishing Ltd, Hersham, Surrey KT12 4RG.
Printed by Ian Allan Printing Ltd, Hersham, Surrey KT12 4RG.

Code: 0404/B

Preface

The Class 50s were the last batch of first-generation diesel locomotives introduced by British Rail under the Modernisation Plan, which saw the demise of steam and the transition to diesel traction. The Class 50 was a locomotive designed by a committee and as built had a host of new gadgets such as inertial filters, rheostatic braking and, more importantly, the first generation of electronic traction control.

My first acquaintance with the class was in the summer of 1969 while I was staying with relatives in Penrith. One day I was standing beside Scout Green 'box on Shap Bank when a pair of them thundered down the bank at high speed on an up express. The sight of these new gleaming machines at speed was to leave a lasting impression.

My first professional involvement came in 1974 when, as a young engineering trainee, I was seconded to Bath Road depot in Bristol. The class had recently been transferred to the Western Region, and I spent a fascinating time learning about the mystique of their electronic control, load-banking locomotives and riding them in service while fault-finding.

Some 15 years later I was, to my surprise, to renew my involvement, when in 1989 I was appointed as Area Fleet Manager based at Laira depot in Plymouth. I was to oversee the final years of their operation and the run-down of the class, involving their gradual withdrawal and in many cases transfer into preservation, and keeping these problematic but charismatic machines in front-line service made for challenging but enjoyable times.

David Clough is recognised as probably one of the foremost authorities on the history of Class 50s, having followed them closely from introduction right through to retirement, and is now actively involved in the preservation movement. In this volume he records the story in detail, but, because he has drawn extensively on the knowledge of professional railwaymen, he has been able to provide an inside view into the development and performance of what was arguably one of the most distinctive classes of locomotive, which found affection not only with rail enthusiasts but also with many of the railwaymen who had the good fortune to work with them.

From a personal perspective I believe Class 50s marked a significant contribution to the development of diesel traction on Britain's railways and paved the way for the development of probably the most successful diesel-electric 'locomotive' – the HST power car. Class 50s were hard work, not only for the staff but also for managers, who had to control the totally unpredictable costs of their operation. They did, however, have character and provided a sense of fun and pride to all those railwaymen who worked with them. When you opened the power handle you were never quite sure what would happen next!

Geoff Hudson
Area Fleet Manager, Plymouth, 1989-96

Introduction

For over 30 years I have been a Class 50 fan – but not a sycophant. This means that, unlike most enthusiasts, I am prepared to recognise weaknesses in my favourite type of locomotive. The following pages chart the history of arguably BR's most controversial class, highlighting weak points as well as the many strengths and successes of the design. Anyone expecting a rose-tinted view will be disappointed, and, for the first time, there will be an honest, in-depth appraisal drawn primarily from official records and the comments of those who lived with Class 50 day in and day out. A significant quantity of material appears here for the first time. Many of the official records that have formed the basis for the text have, sadly, now been destroyed, and my personal archive, accumulated over the last 20 years, has thus proved invaluable.

Over many years I have been privileged to have access to the managers involved in keeping Class 50s working. This book thus records not the recollections of an outsider looking in but the views of insiders expressed to an interested observer. Naturally there will have been a little gilding of the good and glossing over of the bad, but never has there been any attempt to conceal the official statistics, be they good, bad or indifferent. For the first time, the true tale of this enigmatic class is told, warts and all, with no intention of presenting a glorified account as so often portrayed, unjustifiably, about steam locomotives or in other modern-traction texts.

Even in a book of this size, with over 40,000 words, there is insufficient space to be definitive on all aspects of the operating life of the class. Hence very few 'firsts' are described, when the debut was made on a particular line or service. The same applies to last workings too. Instead, the approach taken has been to blend the principal duties performed, how well these were performed in terms of timekeeping and train-running, and the behind-the-scenes issues that BR had to deal with to keep the wheels turning.

For simplicity, I have used the words 'English Electric' (abbreviated to EE), rather than confusing the reader in keeping tabs on the mergers and de-mergers of railway engineering. For the record, EE merged with GEC on 29 November 1968. In the early 1990s GEC merged its power-turbine and railway interests with the French company Alsthom, becoming GEC-Alsthom. Latterly, the company has become simply Alstom, which, in 2003, announced the ending of new-build work in Great Britain. Vulcan Foundry, where the Class 50s were built, finally closed in 2001, with the locomotive works at Preston being run down to provide only repair facilities from 2003. Preston contributed electrical equipment for Class 50 and, with Vulcan, had a distinguished history in railway engineering.

Care has been taken in selecting the illustrations to ensure a fair balance to reflect the operational history. Too often in the past, books have shown few pictures of the LMR era, because the authors wanted to use more of their own, WR-biased photographs. A conscious effort has been made too to include at least one picture of each Class 50. Inevitably, though, some examples have enjoyed far more limelight for various reasons. No 50007, in its distinctive green livery and the last to be withdrawn, and No D400 or 50050, the doyen and next-to-last on BR's books, are two obvious cases. My personal favourite, No 50035, has also proved to be a star. It was the first named and then twinned with the Royal Navy ship after which it was named (in this case *Ark Royal*). It also ran in service in grey primer, and was one of the last two to be allocated at Old Oak Common and the first to be preserved. Photographic evidence also shows it must have been a very reliable performer, because it always seemed to be active. Perhaps in the next couple of years it might also return to the main line.

Writing the manuscript has been a labour of love. Of all the books I have written, this is the one I have always wanted to do, and the publishers have been kind enough to indulge my ideas. I pray that their faith proves justified! The intention has been to enable non-technical readers to understand a little of what makes a Class 50 tick, as well as what caused the ticking to stop. This has meant writing a story rather than a descriptive treatise. Large tables of train-timing figures have been banished for the same reason. Unless otherwise credited, all performance data is my own. Where I have used the work of others to any extent, this has been drawn from reliable recorders, who are credited appropriately.

Many people have contributed in large or small measure, and I append below their names. I trust you, the reader, will find the book interesting. I have drawn on past issues of the Class 50 Society's magazines, almost all of which I contributed to. The three videos produced by Locomaster Profiles, depicting the final years of the class, have been both an evocative reminder of times past, as well as an excellent reference source and are highly recommended.

As already stated, I am delighted to have managed to include a picture of every locomotive dealt with in this book. This embraces all the early prototypes, as well as Portuguese No 1809, the one most enthusiasts missed in traffic. Indeed, one of the rarest illustrations shows No 1803 on an engineer's train near Oporto whilst in original livery. I have used a number of David Canning's pictures. Regrettably, he did not usually note the details and this explains the lack of caption information.

Should you feel moved to correspond, either by way of comment, amplification or in the provision of further material and photographs, please feel free to do so via the publishers.

I am very grateful to Geoff Hudson, who so ably filled the position of Area Fleet Manager at Laira during the last years of the class in BR service, for writing the Preface and providing information that has enriched the text. Jonathan Dunster, my opposite number in the Fifty Fund, has devoted much time to checking and updating my records on last workings, liveries and final TOPS hours. This has enabled comprehensive data to be included in the Appendix. Dates for commissioning, renumbering, works visits and withdrawal comes from original BR sources and may differ from dates published elsewhere. Thanks for assistance provided with this project are also due to Frank Alcock, Martin Beckett, Neville Davies, Barry Evans, Paul Furtek, Chris Holland, Mike Hunt, Geoff Hurst, Peter Meredith, Paul Spracklen, Alec Williams and Mike Woodhouse. Finally, my wife, Jo, has given me considerable support in various aspects of compiling the manuscript and photographic selection.

David Clough
Leigh, September 2003

Bowler hatted Chief Traction Inspector, John Hughes checks for a clear road out of Vulcan Foundry and onto BR tracks for the first time, as No D400 makes its debut. *E. N. Bellass*

EARLY DEVELOPMENT

Any study of Class 50 needs to draw on the history of The English Electric Company's (EE's) involvement in diesel rail traction. The company entered the rail traction market in 1927 when it provided the electrical equipment for a 500hp diesel railcar, built by the London, Midland & Scottish Railway (LMS). In 1934 it produced a diesel engine with a 10in bore, which was designated the 'K' model. The six-cylinder version, 6KT, became the power unit installed in the 350bhp LMS shunters and earned itself a good reputation for reliability and an ability to run for long periods between overhauls.

During World War 2 the Royal Navy wanted a more powerful version of this engine. Redesign work and fitting a turbocharger enabled output per cylinder to be raised to 100hp. The first rail contract for this new version came from the Egyptian State Railways, comprising 49 four-cylinder and 13 16-cylinder variants. It was one of the latter that was used in the first main-line diesel locomotive to run on Britain's railways.

LMS PROTOTYPES

It seems that the LMS was determined to pioneer main-line diesel rail traction once World War 2 had ended. In May 1946 Acting Chief Mechanical Engineer H. G. Ivatt and Sir George Nelson of EE agreed to collaborate on the project. The railway works at Derby was put in overall charge of the project, comprising design and construction. Although the concept of the new locomotive – and the development work which EE had undertaken on its 10in-bore diesel – emulated elements of American practice, several factors imposed limitations on the design. Notable among these was the British loading gauge, which was considerably smaller, and the need to keep the maximum axle load to considerably less than the 28-ton limit permitted in the USA.

Design work was made more difficult because of limitations in the available height within Derby Works to lower the diesel engine inside the locomotive body. To overcome this the sides of the locomotive had to be made removable, and this meant that they could not be load-bearing structures. In turn, this forced the use of a heavier underframe assembly than was able to be used in later designs. Whereas in the USA a bogie wheel arrangement of Bo-Bo or A1A-A1A was used, EE required a Co-Co type. Credit is due to the Derby design office, which produced a very good result. EE experienced some problems in developing the 16-cylinder version of its SVT engine, which was derived from the RK range, and it was not delivered to Derby until May 1947. EE also supplied the electrical machines, comprising main and auxiliary generators and traction motors etc. Notwithstanding, Mr Ivatt was determined that the locomotive would be completed before nationalisation of the railways came into effect on 1 January 1948.

American preference for a nose end was followed because of the perceived need to prevent the traincrew from suffering 'sleeper flutter'. Of course, in the USA the nose end also provided protection for the traincrew during collisions with road vehicles on level crossings – something far more frequent there than in this country. In the LMS design the nose end contained only a compressor and traction-motor blower. Nose-end gangway doors were fitted to enable inter-communication with a second locomotive or the train, but these were rarely used and were always a source of draughts in the cab.

Mr Ivatt succeeded in his objective, and on 8 December 1947 he was able to drive the completed locomotive, numbered 10000, out of the erecting shop for its public debut. It was highly commendable that the overall length was as short and, at 61ft 2in, far less than other early prototypes. Overall weight was 130 tons 12cwt, while the maximum axle load was 22 tons 4cwt – less than that of the largest

LMS Pacifics. No 10000 then went to Euston station for exhibition.

The prototype was subjected to trials around Derby before being assigned express passenger turns between St Pancras and Derby from the spring of 1948. On these it was capable of maintaining the schedules set for the 'Jubilee' class steam engines that were the staple power on the route. No 10001 was completed at Derby Works in July 1948 and took over its sister's diagram while the latter entered works for inspection. From October the pair took up West Coast duties, based at Camden steam shed. Later that year the duo moved back to the Midland line, staying until the Summer 1949 timetable, whereupon they returned to the West Coast.

During the next few years the pair were used both singly and in multiple on the main Anglo-Scottish services. Prevailing schedules were undemanding, and overall time could be kept with a single unit. By now allocated to Willesden, Nos 10000/1 were deployed from Euston to Blackpool, Crewe and Liverpool. Again, one locomotive was found able to keep the train to time. Unreliable steam-heating equipment tended to restrict passenger operation to the summer months, but during the winter

there was no shortage of freight traffic to move. The appearance of two prototype diesels on the Southern Region (SR) brought the decision, in the spring of 1953, to concentrate all four machines there, no doubt to focus experience and operation.

SOUTHERN RAILWAY PROTOTYPES

Postwar the Southern Railway produced a comprehensive plan for modernisation. Full electrification of all routes was considered, but, interestingly, a design was drawn up for a large diesel locomotive. The diesel project proceeded more slowly than was the case on the LMS, but, again, it was to EE that the railway turned for the main components. By the time the engine was ordered, EE had made some improvements to the engine fitted in Nos 10000/1. Among these, Napier turbochargers were fitted, and the 16SVT

was now rated at 1,750bhp. The main generator and traction motors were also of EE manufacture.

One important difference between the Southern's prototypes and those of the LMS was in the bogie design. Whereas the latter had a three-axle arrangement where each axle had a traction motor, this resulted in an axle weight which was higher than the Southern desired. In consequence a four-axle bogie was produced which had an unpowered leading pony truck, reducing the maximum axle load to 18 tons 10cwt for an overall locomotive weight of 135 tons. Although this type of 1-Co bogie was used in several of the early BR classes (40, 44, 45 and 46) to provide a wide route availability, improved construction techniques later meant that overall weight could be reduced and so permit the use of a bogie with all three axles powered. The traction-motor gearing was 52:21, which was high, the intention being to allow a maximum speed of 110mph. This was to facilitate a high-speed service from London to Exeter and Bournemouth.

Ashford Works was responsible for construction, and the first machine, numbered 10201, emerged in December 1950. Following light-engine trials, several runs to London Victoria were made on 28 and 29 December. On 4 January 1951 No 10201 was taken over by the LMR and put to work on the Midland route between St Pancras and Manchester Central. This use proved short-lived, however, because on the 17th the locomotive returned to Ashford for repainting and exhibition at the Festival of Britain site in London.

Sister locomotive No 10202 made its debut in August 1951. The performance of No 10201 in the Peak District had shown its traction-motor gearing to be unsuited to the steep gradient, which caused excessive temperatures in the motor windings. It was therefore unsurprising that No 10202 was not appropriated by the LMR. Instead it was based at Nine Elms shed, hauling trains to Weymouth and Exeter. On 15 October a turbocharger bolt fractured, prior to departure from Waterloo. Avoiding a failure, an EE technician sat astride the (hot) main generator for the whole run so that oil could be fed into the turbocharger.

The planned 110mph running never materialised. Just how fast these prototypes actually ran is not known, but certainly the large Bulleid Pacifics were timed at up to 100mph on the Exeter road. A demonstration high-speed trip was arranged for 24 October during which 100mph was sanctioned by the Chief Civil Engineer, but as it turned out the Railway Executive cancelled the run following a series of major failures with a steam locomotive. In the event an eight-coach train ran from Salisbury to London at an average of 60mph and with a 92mph top speed.

No 10201 returned to service in November 1951 after exhibition. The two prototypes continued to operate out of Waterloo, both to Bournemouth/Weymouth and to Exeter. For a spell No 10202 made two return trips a day to Exeter – roughly 4,100 miles per week. Defects with traction motors and the train-heating boiler were the main problems experienced in service. In April 1952 dynamometer-car trials with No 10202 largely verified the operational experience gained with the type. Perhaps the main consequence was the decision to alter the traction-motor gearing to 65:17. This was done during a visit to Brighton Works when the engine was overhauled, this having run for 3,000 hours and the locomotive 100,000 miles. More trials in October demonstrated that the lower gearing gave more tractive effort at lower

Left: **The ex-LMS prototypes did not spend all their time on top-link diagrams. For a spell they found employment on stopping trains between Euston and Bletchley. No 10001 leaves Leighton Buzzard on 7 May 1955 with the 09.10 from Euston.** *David N. Clough collection*

Below: **The Southern prototypes had two spells on the LMR. During the first, No 10201 departs Derby in January 1951 on the 12.05 to St Pancras.** *T. Lakin*

speeds, at the expense of less at higher speeds. Maximum tractive effort was 37,800lb, against the 48,000lb calculated theoretically by EE.

In March 1954 the third prototype, No 10203, fitted with the Mk II version of the 16SVT diesel, made its debut from Brighton Works. Among other enhancements was the use of a four-valve cylinder head and a redesigned connecting rod, which allowed engine speed to be increased from 750 to 850rpm; in consequence the gross output became 2,000bhp.

Dynamometer-car trials showed that, by virtue of its extra power, No 10203 needed to spend less time under load on any given journey than did No 10202, that it was a coach better in haulage power and that it was slightly more fuel-efficient in terms of diesel consumed per drawbar horsepower. However, even No 10203 fell short of what a Bulleid Pacific could achieve in performance terms. Under test conditions an unrebuilt 'Merchant Navy' was able to produce between 150 to 200hp more at the drawbar than No 10203 across the main speed range. With this information the SR decided to retain its fleet of modern Pacifics until extension of electrification could be funded, and so lost interest in main-line diesel traction.

FINAL YEARS

It was perhaps unsurprising that the SR decided to abandon further involvement with main-line diesel traction from 1955, when all five locomotives were reallocated to the LMR, as prior to this there had been a spell when only one of the five machines was in traffic. Based now at Willesden, they worked expresses from Euston to Wolverhampton, Manchester, Glasgow and Perth as well as locals to Bletchley. On the Anglo-Scottish turns Nos 10000/1 were used in multiple, as were Nos 10201/2 on occasions.

Long periods were spent in one or other of the railway's works over the years, 1956 seeing little action from any of the prototypes. This was due partly to the difficulty of obtaining spares and partly to a lack of familiarity with diesel traction among depot staff. Moreover, steam-shed conditions and facilities provided a bad environment in which to operate diesel traction. However, when they were not in works the diesels amassed some very creditable mileages. Figures for the nine-month period ended 30 September 1957 yielded individual mileages of between 74,866 and 111,513, with an average across the five of 91,000 – equivalent to an annual 120,000. This figure stands comparison with mileages accumulated by most BR diesels. In contrast the LMR 'Duchess' Pacifics (on the highest-mileage turns of any steam type on that Region) averaged 56,800 miles, whilst the other principal passenger classes turned in figures of between 41,314 and 45,503 miles.

By the turn of the decade the LMR was receiving a steady flow of new EE Type 4s

Completing a record of each of the Southern's three prototypes, No 10202 sets off for Euston from Crewe on 21 July 1962 during its second period of operation on the LMR.
Brian Haresnape

(Class 40), which shared many major components with No 10203. This impacted on the utilisation of the five prototypes, which began to be confined to London-suburban turns. In December 1962 Nos 10201/3 were dumped at Derby Works, followed soon after in 1963 by No 10000 and No 10202. No 10001 had been the last to receive a works overhaul and remained in traffic until March 1966. A range of design faults across all components occurred during the years, though none was major. This experience was invaluable to EE in refining its equipment, and undoubtedly helped make the 'D200s' more successful. All five prototypes were scrapped in the late 1960s.

THE QUEST FOR MORE POWER

Following on from the success of the early prototypes, when the British Transport Commission (BTC) announced its Pilot Scheme for the elimination of steam traction, EE was a natural choice of supplier for new equipment. Initially, this came in the shape of the Type 1 (Class 20) and Type 4 (Class 40), which employed respectively eight- and 16-cylinder versions of the Mk II SVT engine. The Mk II engine would remain in production until superceded in 1971 by the Mk III, later fitted in Class 56. It was therefore at 2,000hp that EE continued to supply the engine in Class 40, partly because the Class 40's main generator could not handle

higher power, EE preferring to spend its development resources on what turned out to be ill-starred new engines.

In contrast, although Sulzer's LDA engine as fitted to the BR Derby Type 4 (Class 44) of the Pilot Scheme was rated at 2,300hp, by the time the second batch of this type (Class 45) was ordered a couple of years later, development work by Sulzer had brought an improvement to 2,500hp. This widening gap between the Sulzer and EE diesels was not helping the latter win friends in the right places in BR.

Although most of the research budget had gone into new projects, limited capital was made available during this period for enhancements to the Mk II SVT. When, in January 1959, the BTC ordered from EE a new medium-power Type 3 locomotive (to become Class 37), the engine to be used was a charge-cooled version of the Mk II SVT, designated CSVT. Fitting intercoolers pushed up the output per cylinder from 125 to 167hp, and in 12-cylinder form this offered 2,025hp. In the event, the BTC asked for a rating of no more than 1,750bhp. The first EE Type 3 was delivered in December 1960. Meanwhile, on 15 January that year, the BTC had announced that it was seeking a new large Type 4 2,700bhp diesel-electric machine, with both steam and electric train-heating capability.

On 25 May 1961 EE unveiled its 16CSVT, offering 2,700bhp at 167hp per cylinder.

By this time the 12-cylinder version had been in traffic in EE Type 3s for some 16 months. However, although robust, this was always a big, crude powerplant, unlike its Sulzer counterpart, and it was this unfavourable comparison (despite the former being cheap and the latter expensive) that swayed the opinion of the BTC's Chief Mechanical Engineer.

DP2 EMERGES

By May 1961 EE was working on a design which met the BTC requirement for a new Type 4. At the time, the company was preoccupied with producing the Class 55 'Deltics' as well as fulfilling other main-line orders for home and overseas use. It was also road-testing its gas-turbine prototype, GT3. However, it was a very large concern, with more works facilities than any other company. The most expeditious – and cheapest – answer was to use the jigs for a Class 55 bodyshell to accommodate the new 16CSVT engine.

DP2 made its debut on the BR network in May 1962. Most of its superstructure, its cab layout and its bogies were identical to those of a 'Deltic'. Within the engine room, however, the arrangement was more akin to a Class 37, because one large engine and generator set was fitted instead of two smaller ones. The radiators and radiator fan were located at the free end of the engine, and louvres were cut in the bodyside to provide an airflow for cooling purposes. These louvres were thermostatically controlled, unlike on Class 37. Weight, in working order, was 105 tons – six tons heavier than a Class 55 but slightly lighter than a Class 37.

The close similarity to existing EE classes helped DP2 win favour with the operating department, because the need for additional driver training was minimal. The external styling did not, however, conform to the BTC's new thinking, which required a flat cab front. Maximum speed is quoted as 90mph – the same as Class 37 – although the traction motors and gearing were identical to those fitted to both Class 37 and Class 55.

A drab all-over dark green livery was used initially, revised later to two-tone 'Deltic' green. Whilst the Brush prototype *Falcon* and BRCW prototype *Lion* both received BR numbers, DP2 did not. The story of why it did not bear a name has been told before, but, for the record, EE planned to use *Enterprise* but another British prototype received this title before EE could bestow it on its new creation. When *Challenger* was suggested, an EE director called a halt to the naming process, asserting that the other prototypes were the 'challengers'. Instead the internal working name of Diesel Prototype 2, in abbreviated form, was used.

TO TRAFFIC

On 2 May 1962 DP2 made a proving trip from Vulcan Foundry, Newton-le-Willows, where it was built, to Chester and back.

Below: **English Electric produced DP2 in response to the BTC's call for a 2,700bhp locomotive. It was based initially at Camden shed for working a diagram from Euston to Liverpool Lime Street and is seen here passing Wolverton with the up 'Manxman' (14.05 ex Liverpool) on 21 July 1962.** *J. C. Haydon*

Below right: **DP2's driving position and controls matched those of the 'Deltics'. Note the grouping of the cab instruments.** *EE*

This was to check instrumentation and general fitness to run. Following some tests and adjustments undertaken at Vulcan Foundry and BR's Crewe Works, on the 8th it took a 475-ton test train from Crewe to Penrith and back. Three days later crew training between Euston and Birmingham began from Camden shed, and entry into revenue service followed on the 14th.

Initial running was between Euston and Liverpool Lime Street. Of course, West Coast upgrading and electrification work was underway, and this, coupled with the fact that schedules were based around the existing 2,000bhp EE Type 4, meant that timings were not taxing for so powerful a machine as DP2. From the Winter 1962 timetable DP2 moved onto a Euston–Carlisle diagram, involving the 1.25pm down and 1.25am up, which accumulated a similar weekly mileage. From Summer 1963 came a fresh set of turns, this time to Blackpool on the 5.5pm down and 8.0am up.

EASTERN REGION

Several factors may have brought about DP2's move to the Eastern Region (ER) when Vulcan finished its 5,000-hours overhaul in July 1963. At the time, electrification of the WCML through to

After overhaul at Vulcan in 1965 DP2 gave up its drab dark-green livery for two-tone 'Deltic' styling. On 3 August 1965 it leaves King's Cross at the head of the down 'Sheffield Pullman'. *EE*

13

Glasgow seemed certain, whilst EE wanted a more challenging set of schedules than the LMR could offer. Now based at the new Finsbury Park depot, DP2 worked to Leeds and back on 13 July before taking up King's Cross 'Deltic' No 7 diagram from the 15th. This encompassed the 10.10am to Edinburgh and 10.30pm return, loaded to around 450 tons.

With the end of the summer timetable and consequently the need to deputise for a shortage of Class 55s, DP2 was used on the 'Master Cutler' from King's Cross to Sheffield. This was a lightly loaded train, normally handled by a Class 37. In April 1965 DP2 entered Vulcan Foundry for overhaul after completing 380,000 miles in roughly three years. It emerged in standard Class 55 two-tone green and from 14 June was allocated to Tinsley depot, Sheffield. It now made two return trips on weekdays from Sheffield to King's Cross, the last on the 23.20 Tinsley–King's Cross goods, with a return run from the capital to Doncaster on Saturdays. On 13 August, however, there was a reallocation back to Finsbury Park, although the trains worked remained the same.

CLASS 50 PROTOTYPE

In 1965 British Rail ordered 50 Type 4s of a new design from EE. DP2 was to serve as a testbed for the electronic control system to be used in the new design. It was taken out of service on 31 January 1966 and sent to Vulcan for a 3,000-hours engine exam, plus installation of said control system. Thus fitted, from 20 June it hauled the car carrier between Holloway and Edinburgh. However, the end of the summer timetable meant the car-carrier diagram finished, and during October DP2 was to be found on King's Cross–Cambridge duties.

Further prototype testing of features to be used in the new design saw EE engineers install additional equipment at Finsbury Park during November 1966. By now the ER had entered into a contract with EE to pay for the use of the locomotive, and both parties wanted to ensure it accumulated high mileages. To this end, from 2 January 1967, to increase the miles run, DP2 worked the 12.00 to Edinburgh and 22.30 return – 4,500 miles per week – and the trains covered by this diagram (which took in a trip to Leeds) constituted the locomotive's regular work for the remainder of its operating life.

Additional proving of the new slow-speed-control system for working 'merry-go-round' coal trains resulted in DP2's going to Doncaster. On 28 January, using the new electronics, it hauled a 1,648-ton train up an incline of 1 in 200. On wet rails, DP2 struggled to get on the move due to repeated wheelslip; using the new tractive-effort control, the tendency to slip was reduced – the low-speed electronic wheelslip-protection system was able to arrest wheelslip very rapidly. (The success of these features should be borne in mind in relation to similar trials carried out in October 1987 with No 50149.)

DP2 returned to traffic on 1 February on the 12.00 to Edinburgh. Although records of several runs behind the locomotive have been published, most are on the lightly loaded Sheffield trains. However, it seems that that DP2 was able to maintain contemporary 'Deltic' schedules and also run at 100mph. From details of a Newcastle–Edinburgh journey published by Cecil J. Allen in 1967, it is clear that the full rated output of 2,700bhp was being developed.

On 31 July DP2 was heading north of York on its booked turn when it collided with derailed cement wagons. The resulting damage was severe and it came off the ER's locomotive allocation on 9 September. EE considered repairing the damage, but eventually the proposal was abandoned. DP2 languished at Vulcan until 1970, when it was cannibalised, with components going into the Class 50 pool. Its 16CSVT engine went initially into No 417 but finished its working life in No 50037 – suffering a major failure in September 1991 and bringing about that locomotive's withdrawal – before being dumped in No 50023.

DP2 accumulated 607,300 miles in just over five years – an exceptional feat for a prototype. In its last 12 months of operation it averaged 19,000 miles per casualty. Whilst this is a very good figure, it should be borne in mind that DP2 was accompanied in service by an EE technician, who would have been able to resolve problems beyond the wit of a driver and thus keep the locomotive operational. Maintenance was also handled by EE staff, who would almost certainly have shown greater care in critical areas than would have been the case with routine BR depot repairs.

2 The Class 50 Contract

With DP2 so successful, EE must have felt frustrated to be missing out on repeat orders from BR for 2,750bhp locomotives. In an article for a *Railway World Annual* in the late 1970s, Roger Ford gave an outline of how events turned EE's way in 1965. Mr Ford observed that in early 1965 the Regional lobby identified a need for between 50 and 112 additional large Type 4s, but the BR Board was unconvinced. An enquiry was issued calling for tenders based on the BR/Brush Type 4 design with either a Sulzer 12LDA28C or EE 16CSVT diesel powerplant. BR's call for an alternative diesel was because stress cracks were coming to light with the former unit and it wanted to keep its options open.

Official records show EE submitted its tender on 2 June, but Mr Ford says this lapsed. Not too long afterwards it became clear that sanction for extension of WCML electrification north of Weaver Junction to Glasgow would not be forthcoming in the foreseeable future. This left a shortfall in diesel power for this route, such that most services were still timed for steam locomotives or the 2,000bhp EE Type 4s. Something more powerful was needed.

Knowing that BR's finances were tight and that Government sanction for major capital projects was in doubt, EE used some lateral thinking. It was keen to keep production going at Vulcan, and political lobbying was applied in support of an order for the works. It was already leasing its new large computers to industry, so why not offer to lease locomotives to BR? Leasing had the advantage of spreading the cost over the term of the lease, in a similar way to hire purchase. In terms of Government finance, however, leasing costs were treated as revenue expenditure rather than capital outlay, and this allowed them to be treated in a different way. A further sweetener was added to EE's proposal: based on DP2's performance, the company offered an availability guarantee (not, as sometimes thought, a maintenance

agreement), whereby a penalty would be payable to BR if fewer than 42 locomotives (84%) were available for traffic each day. This figure assumed two locomotives would be undergoing works overhauls and that five would be on routine maintenance at any one time, allowing one 'spare' for unplanned repair, making eight out of traffic. Faced with such an attractive proposal, BR signed a letter of intent on 12 November 1965 for 50 100mph locomotives, and thus EE contract No CCT1421 was initiated.

Frames for a Class 50 note that initial filling out was with the frames inverted. *EE*

Above: **Squadron construction was clearly well underway by the time this view of the body frame for one machine was recorded.** *EE*

Above right: **A Class 50 bogie ready to slot under a body, set amidst several partly completed examples.** *EE*

Somewhere along the line EE's idea of producing 50 production series DP2s, with redesigned body, went out of the window. Roger Ford says BR referred to the new design as the BR/EE Type 4 in a similar way to its adoption of BR/Brush Type 4 for the 'D1500' design. EE files give a brief description of the new fleet on the day of the letter of intent, and this shows dual braking, electric train heat (ETH) and dynamic (or rheostatic) braking as in the specification.

The ER at Doncaster Works was to supervise the design and inspect building work. Among the BR headquarters engineers was Walter Jowett, an ex-EE man, who was to play an important part in the thinking behind what emerged as the BR/EE Type 4.

CONTRACT AND SPECIFICATION

Dated 25 August 1967, the contract covering the locomotives was unique in BR history in comprising an agreement to manufacture and an agreement to hire. The former was between BR and EE, whilst the latter was between BR and English Electric Leasings Ltd (an EE subsidiary), with the latter buying the 50 machines from EE. A price of £120,930 per locomotive was agreed initially, but during the delivery period this rose to £128,000 due to permitted inflation and modifications. The period of the primary lease was seven years, with an option to extend into a secondary lease thereafter. Hire charges (or rental payments – the term used in the contract) were:

1. 24 quarterly payments of 4.326% of the locomotive value
2. One payment of 24.404% of the locomotive value
3. One payment of 0.375% of the locomotive value

The first Payment 1 and Payment 3 were made on the first day of the month following the month each locomotive was accepted by BR and the hire period commenced. If the hire commenced after the 19th of a month then EE had to wait an extra month for these revenues. Payment 2 was not due until three months after the hire period had ended. If Bank base rate (then known as the discount rate) fluctuated either side of 6% then the rate of payments 1 above also varied. At the end of the primary lease period BR could opt for a secondary lease of indefinite length at a nominal £50 per quarter per locomotive, but there was no provision for BR to buy because this would have caused difficulty for EE in claiming tax relief on the assets it was leasing.

The contract goes into a lot more detail about responsibilities on both sides, but these really go beyond the scope of this book. Possible exceptions are, however, the requirement for the carrying of a small bodyside plate that stated that the locomotive was on hire from English Electric Leasings Ltd and also the delivery schedule. Deliveries were contracted to start in July 1967 and be completed in June 1968.

The agreement included a guarantee that not less than 84% of the delivered fleet (after delivery of the 25th example) would be available for traffic at 09.00 each day during the term of the primary lease. If less than 84% were available, then a penalty of £50 per day per locomotive below 84% was payable by EE to BR. Excluded from the calculation was any locomotive that was out of service due to BR's fault. Included in this category would be defects due to collision or derailment damage or due to the agreed level of spares not being on hand.

Appended to the contract was the standard technical specification – DE/4/5 – which had been compiled by the BTC in April 1960. Supplementing this was a technical specification for the new Type 4s, and this detailed variations from DE/4/5. It makes clear which party (BR or EE) had initiated which features. Added at BR's request were:

- Provision to operate up to three locomotives in multiple, though only two examples were to be equipped initially with external jumper connections
- Dual braking equipment
- Slow-speed control (SSC) between 0 and 3mph for operating merry-go-round (MGR) trains
- Push/pull control gear
- Dynamic braking

Jointly, BR and EE decided to fit inertial filtration equipment and use steel instead of aluminium for the fuel tank. The tank had a capacity of 1,000 gallons – a useful uplift from the 810gal tank fitted to the BR/Brush Type 4. These changes increased overall weight to 117 tons and maximum axle load from the DE/4/5 limit of 19 tons to 19 tons 10cwt.

A few improvements had been made to the design of the 16CSVT since the unit (IH5567) installed in DP2 was built. These were:

- Thick web crankshaft in 50-ton ultra-tensile steel
- Woodward governor with fuel-limiting device
- Detachable exhaust-manifold-bellows assemblies between each line
- Improved flexible drive to oil and water pumps
- Camshaft chain with force-fit links

Regrettably, the improvements did not include dispensing with camshaft chain drive because this had a tendency to stretch, and engine timing suffered in consequence. Use of a hand-operated lubricating-oil-priming pump was a departure from DE/4/5. This meant that priming a cold engine with oil still had to be done by the driver using a hand pump, with the risk that he might not bother and the engine would run devoid of oil initially. Here was an example of penny-pinching to save money. The engine had four turbochargers, one mounted at each corner; using four, instead of two larger ones, was necessary because of the restricted loading gauge on BR.

Attached to the engine at No 2 end was the Type EE840/4B main generator. Hung on this, in turn, was the ETH generator and auxiliary generator. The ETH generator complied with DE/4/5 in supplying 320kW at 800V. Later BR coaching stock used 850V systems, and 320kW also proved to be a little low when air-conditioned coaches started to be introduced. Taken with the higher voltage demanded, these factors put a strain on the ETH generator, to its detriment. With 320kW output, this permitted a maximum BR ETH index of 61, once power for the radiator fan is taken into account. By contrast, when ETH was fitted to other diesel locomotives in later years, the ETH index was 66 and the ETH generator ran at 850V.

An EE KV10 electronic-field-supply unit, one for each generator, controlled both the main and ETH generators. The use of

16CSVT power unit, ready for use. This is actually the engine from DP2. *Martin Beckett*

electronics gave greater precision and a quicker response over conventional technology. It also allowed the provision of a control for the driver to select a desired tractive effort, in addition to the usual control of horsepower by the driver's power handle. The main purpose of the driver's tractive-effort control was to impose an upper, sustainable limit on tractive effort when rail adhesion was poor. Being a more precise control than the power handle, this allowed the driver to minimise the risk of wheelslip. Two automatic wheelslip-protection systems were installed. For low-speed protection a current-balance system monitored any imbalance in the current of the six traction motors and cut power as required. For higher-speed wheelslip control a motor-voltage-balance system operated in a similar way. A traditional (and slow-acting) Westinghouse anti-slip brake was also provided.

The six traction motors were mounted on two three-axle bogies. They were very similar to – and interchangeable with – those used in the EE Type 3 and 5 designs (Classes 37 and 55) and were connected in three series pairs. Three stages of field-weakening permitted full engine output to be available between 15 and 87mph. Bogie design was also similar to earlier EE designs.

A Hawker Siddeley Dynamics solid-state temperature-sensing device controlled the motor for the radiator fan drive as well as the air-operated radiator shutters. The motor ran at three speeds and had a stop condition. Its speed (and hence rotational speed of the radiator fan) was determined by the cooling demand from the engine. EE had planned to use the Sulzer coupling arrangement to drive the radiator fan from the free end of the engine, as used in DP2 and the 'D6700' Type 3 (Class 37). BR asked for a redesign, using a motor drive, similar to that fitted in the BR/Crompton Parkinson 'D11' series (Class 45).

Instead of the traditional 'dead man's pedal', which drivers had to keep depressed during motion, an electronically controlled driver's safety device was fitted. This comprised a three-position foot pedal and a push button. Drivers had to keep the pedal in the mid position and respond to a periodic bleep by either depressing or releasing the pedal or pushing the button. This novel feature at the time earned the Class 50s their first nickname of 'Bleeps'.

BR wanted the fitting of push/pull equipment to enable a locomotive to be driven remotely from a coach fitted with a driving cab. Its Doncaster office had already produced a system for fitting to the EE Type 3s.

Dynamic braking had also not been installed before in a BR main-line diesel, although it was becoming a feature in the USA and continues there on current designs. The system had, of course, been used in electric locomotives in Britain for some time. It uses the traction motors, controlled by the main generator, to retard movement as an alternative to traditional friction brakes. By virtue of their rotation during movement, the traction motors generate an electromotive force in opposition to the direction of movement. It is this force that is harnessed for braking purposes. Naturally the energy produced by the traction motors had to be dissipated in some way. It was fed into banks of resistances and these had roof-level louvres that opened to provide cooling air when dynamic braking was in use.

The control system blended the locomotive air-brake system between these speeds to provide a constant brake effort that corresponded to the effort of the train brakes. Maximum dynamic-braking effort occurred at 26.5mph and was effectively nil by 11mph. Dynamic braking offers a saving in brake-gear maintenance –

Driver's control desk in original condition. From left to right, the gauges are: air-pipe-brake-pressure gauge, bogie-brake-pressure gauge, train-vacuum-pressure gauge, speedometer (0-120mph), current-limit-setting unit, main ammeter (power and dynamic brake), speedometer (0-3mph), slow-speed-setting unit and main-reservoir-pressure gauge. *BR*

provided this is not offset by problems with the dynamic-braking equipment.

Two rolled-steel joists formed the underframe, tied by fabricated cross-members. The top of the underframe was plated and sealed so that any fuel, oil or water which spilled inside the locomotive did not leak onto the track but was collected in a spillage tank. A flat-ended type of superstructure was provided, with separate, removable roof panels for each internal section of the locomotive, viz radiator compartment, filter compartment, engine room, control cubicle and dynamic brake resistances. Provision for retro-fitting sanding gear was made in the shape of bodyside fillers and sandboxes inside the superstructure.

Maximum design speed was given as 105mph, but this was limited in service to 100mph. Maximum tractive effort was 48,500lb and was limited to this by a maximum main-generator current of 2,400A; overload protection for the main generator cut in at 2,700A. At the main generator's continuous-rating output of 1,800A the tractive effort was 33,000lb at a speed of 18mph. This provided 2,070hp at the rail (rhp), equal to 76.7% of engine output. This was a lower level of efficiency than on other large Type 4s, with the 'D1500s' turning in an efficiency of 78.5% and the 'D11s' 80%.

The above provides an outline of the salient features of the locomotive as built. A full technical description can be found in the chapters written by Michael Hunt in *Class 50s at Work* by John Vaughan, published by Ian Allan.

DESIGN EVOLUTION

Once BR issued its letter of intent, detailed planning of the project began within EE, co-ordinated by the Traction Sales & Contracts Department, based at Bradford. Component construction was, as usual, split between several constituent parts of EE. The mechanical parts, naturally, were down to Vulcan. Electrical machines fell to Preston, whilst Rugby made the engines (for assembly at Preston or Vulcan), and Bradford was to produce traction-motor gear-wheels and pinions.

By 9 February 1966 the Vulcan drawing office had completed detailed drawings for external and internal arrangements. As regards the cab-front styling, this was not an end to the matter. Three parties were

Aerial view of complete locomotive (D406), with radiator fan to the left on the floor. *EE*

involved in the process – BR, BR's stylist and EE. The BR Derby Works staff produced a mock-up of one proposal, whilst EE's Bradford works did likewise for an alternative. The latter featured a wrap-around windscreen, similar to that used on the Trans-Pennine DMUs, with the box for the train reporting number set below the windscreens; this was rejected by BR. By 26 April 1966 John Dowling, CMEE at Vulcan, reported to his Bradford colleagues that matters on cab-front design were settled and that the Derby mock-up was being followed, further input from the stylist being irrelevant. The reporting-number box was moved to above the windscreen to allow for the fitting of multiple-unit jumpers at waist level; on older classes these were at buffer-beam height.

In February 1966 Vulcan's Estimating Department was still working on an adjusted price for the revised locomotive. Mr Dowling was coming under pressure

No D434 being lowered onto its bogies. *EE*

from EE's Bradford Traction Sales office over costs. In a rebuttal memorandum of 28 March 1966 he admitted that the new design was 'challenging' and bore little resemblance to the original EE tender. Such was the way BR now involved itself in design details. Clearly there was a battle between autonomous parts of EE, because a memo of 17 June from Vulcan to Bradford is uncompromising; it states that Vulcan had quoted in April 1965 for 50 DP2s and that the present locomotive was markedly different for reasons that were to everyone's satisfaction. Politely, it states that Bradford had better accept Vulcan's revised quote for an order vital to both Bradford and Vulcan.

At Preston, development engine IH4981 had continued to be used for proving purposes and had run at up to 3,300bhp output. For some reason, however, main-generator production had been switched from there to Bradford, and deliveries commenced much later than planned. This then held up testing of the engines that were to be fitted into individual locomotives: instead of engine-and-generator sets being shipped to Vulcan from the autumn of 1966, in the event none was ready until the spring of 1967.

EE had identified some problems with the traditional oil-wetted primary filtration panels for the engine room when these were applied in conjunction with the (then) latest uprated diesels. The uprating was through higher turbocharger performance, and these needed an air input at moderate temperature. High engine output brought higher ambient air temperature in the engine room, so air management was becoming crucial; DP2's bodyside windows were usually left open during running to improve air flow. The traditional oil-wetted filters tended to have their oil sucked out and into the turbocharger air intakes, which was far from ideal.

The BR Design Panel clearly wanted to move towards a sleek, unbroken bodyside, so opening windows and large filter bank intake grilles were out. In fact BR also wanted a sealed roof. On 13 December 1965 Mr Dowling set out his thoughts on Mr Jowett's dislike of the air ducts that EE had found essential on DP2. From the surviving correspondence, it seems EE first floated the idea of having inertial filters as the primary method of engine room air filtration. EE had limited experience of this type of filter, which had been used in a recent design for East Africa, but inertial filters were used extensively in the USA. The principle of the system relies on passing air through a maze, and each turn in the maze disrupts the flow. By virtue of having a mass heavier than air, dirt particles then drop out because of this disruption. A big advantage is that inertial filters are supposedly virtually maintenance-free – initially higher in cost but offering long-term savings in service. However, employing this system increased the locomotive's underframe length (by 3ft) as well as overall weight. Latterly Mr Dowling admitted to being backed into a corner by BR over air filtration, with inertial filters as the only option. He found BR to be very conservative on this subject.

EE used a pressurised engine room in conjunction with inertial filters. This was to keep unfiltered air out of the locomotive interior. Two inertial filters were used, one at each end of the engine compartment. The main one was positioned over the generators, and the noise of air passing over the filter gills resulted in the Class 50s' being nicknamed 'Hoovers' in later years by Paddington station staff.

Curiously, the contract technical specification makes no mention of the inclusion of weight-transfer-compensation equipment. When a heavy train is started, a locomotive tends to tilt backwards slightly. This means adhesion weight on the leading axles is reduced, and there is an increased risk of slipping. Whilst BR expressed an interest in trialling this system, EE already had a budget for its development as part of its proposed 4,000bhp diesel scheme and was looking for a locomotive on which to fit it. Thus, whilst making provision on all the class for retro-fitting fell to BR, EE paid for the equipment installed on No D417, the locomotive selected for the in-service trial.

EE had for some time been working on the development of electronic control systems for rail traction. Initially this work had been with electric locomotives and multiple-unit stock, and a natural progression was to fit such systems into diesel-electric locomotives – initially four EE Type 3s based at Stratford depot. The new Type 4 offered a chance for fleet use of an electronic control system, and DP2 provided the test vehicle as development of the production version progressed. The development team faced quite a daunting task to engineer a full control system that encompassed the loading on the diesel engine, control of all three generators, radiator-fan control and wheelslip protection, not to mention BR's request for dynamic braking, slow-speed control and push/pull operation.

A closed-loop system was devised which can be seen as the basis for the system used in BR's High Speed Train power cars. The system's 'brain' – the current- and load-control unit, designated CU1 – receives signals from and issues signals to all the parts of the system and controls the KV10 units (CU3 and CU6) that govern main- and ETH-generator excitation. Of course, compared to today's technology these electronic units appear akin to dinosaurs, in terms of both size and functionality. Although they worked fairly well after a settling-in period, they presented a challenge for maintenance staff who were totally new to their concepts.

From the high-tech to the low-tech. As on its earlier, 'D200' Type 4s, EE provided a semi-rotary hand pump in the radiator compartment to facilitate emergency refilling of the radiators. A bucket was standard equipment for this purpose. This combination was replicated on Class 50, and there are at least two known instances of the driver of a stricken locomotive, overheated due to lack of coolant, heading off across the fields with his bucket in search of water. Thus a failure was averted; such simple methods sometimes offer perfect solutions.

Under the BR/EE contract, the first two locomotives were to be handed over in July, with production rising to five per

BR wanted a sealed locomotive. Here No D400 is put under a water-sprinkler at Vulcan to test for leaks. *EE*

month to complete deliveries in June 1968. Further slippage came about because Bradford could not produce generators quickly enough, possibly due to a labour dispute. A second revision to the delivery timetable now envisaged deliveries spanning the period August 1967–August 1968. By the beginning of March 1967 only two complete power units had gone to Vulcan after full testing.

Engine testing in No D400 was still in progress in early August, when a meeting was called to discuss perceived inadequacies in the cooling system; basically, the engine was running too hot. Some tweaking of the cooling system had helped, but a 1% (25bhp) engine derating was put forward. If the slight derating of the engine were not implemented, the cooling system might not be able to dissipate the engine heat, but BR was not told of this. The meeting decided to stick with the 2,700bhp figure and encourage regular cleaning of radiator panels.

On 19 August No D400 moved under its own power for the first time; by 4 September it was passed by BR as fit to run beyond the confines of Vulcan Foundry and made the customary light-engine trip to Chester and back. This was to check instrumentation and ensure that everything worked satisfactorily and was the norm for all Vulcan-built locomotives. Construction was thus behind even the revised timetable; in fact, No 449 did not leave Vulcan until 30 November 1968. This delay may have caused the final withdrawal of steam locomotives to be deferred by several months, until August, because the diesels to be cascaded to replace steam could not be re-diagrammed until sufficient of the new Type 4s were in traffic. EE had to pay BR £213,142 in liquidated damages for the late delivery – a costly overrun.

Livery for the Class 50s was BR Rail Blue for roof and bodysides, black for the buffer-beams, undergear and bogies and yellow for the cab fronts. Numbering was in the range D400-49. All 50 examples were outshopped carrying the 'D' prefix to their running number, even though this had officially been dropped by the time No 437 was commissioned on 20 September 1968, following the demise of main-line steam.

First outing on BR: No D400 on its first proving run. Arthur Amson is in the secondman's seat, and the LMR's Chief Traction Inspector, John Hughes, is just visible in the cab. *EE*

3

The Early Years

COMMISSIONING AND DRIVER TRAINING

No D400 set off from Vulcan for Crewe and its commissioning trials on 11 September 1967. Next day it made two return trips from Crewe to Stafford, hauling 15 coaches, for a 100mph trial. Apparently it managed the speed – but only just. On the 13th came a maximum-load trial over Shap and Beattock which involved taking a 1,000-ton oil train from Stanlow oil refinery to Dalmarnock, Glasgow. The 15th saw a 450-ton loose-coupled freight worked between Bamfurlong sorting sidings, Wigan, and Hellifield, with a repeat run on the 20th. A planned test of the slow-speed-control system at Basford Hall, Crewe, appears not to have taken place. A number of minor shakedown points emerged but nothing serious. During the trials, which both BR and EE considered a success, the engine shut down unintentionally four or five times. Tripping of the train-heat generator's over-voltage relay (HOVR) was suspected. (Such shutdowns still happen to this day.) On the 22nd No D400 returned to Vulcan for rectification.

On 5 October EE's Tommy Wrighton delivered the third and final commissioning report on No D400, which had returned to Crewe from Vulcan on 27 September after modification. The trip had been made on 2 October from Crewe to Carlisle via Hellifield with 17 coaches weighing 643 tons. Train heat was used for 30 minutes on the down run and throughout on the return. Although a few minor matters were noted, BR issued an acceptance certificate, and No D400 became available for crew training.

Sensibly, BR had based a technical representative at Vulcan during No D400's construction, in order to get to grips with every aspect of the design. Arthur Amson from Crewe had his own office and was even used by EE to train its staff on the class. When No D400 arrived at Crewe, Mr Amson led the training of both depot and footplate staff.

As part of the commissioning trials, on 13 September 1967 No D400 hauled a 1,000-ton train of oil tanks from Stanlow to Dalmarnock in Glasgow. It returned the next day and is seen passing Frodsham, near journey's end.
C. R. Whitfield

EE sensibly arranged to station technicians at the depots where the class was most likely to be stopped for both routine and unscheduled maintenance. Most important was the Crewe-based representative, because the LMR chose to recall locomotives to home base for anything beyond minor attention, at least initially. EE's site rep there was responsible for collating a lot of information that would assist in all aspects of contract management. Included in these reports were commissioning details, faults, work carried out by both him and BR, availability figures and also a reporting-back function on views and concerns expressed by BR. Carlisle Kingmoor and Glasgow Polmadie depots also had a technician on site, both of whom also filed incident reports. Taken together, the surviving records from these three depots provide a fascinating insight into the early life of the class. Whilst most of the information in the report logs is, by necessity, of a technical nature, nevertheless a picture can be established of how 'D400' operations gradually spread from No D400's first arrival at Crewe until the 50 machines dominated all aspects of train running across North West England and Central and Southern Scotland.

Alan Chamberlain filed the first Crewe site report for the week ending 7 October and later joined the LMR's CM&EE Department at Derby, thus continuing his involvement with the class. Sadly, he died a number of years ago. No D400 spent 4 October undergoing a 'B' exam on Crewe depot and thereafter was used for training motive-power inspectors and footplate staff, both on the depot and between Crewe and Rhyl on empty coaching stock. The only problem reported was the engine shutting down when the driver moved the power controller rapidly from intermediate to full power.

By the following week T. E. Cottam had filed the site report, and he became the EE representative at Crewe depot for several years. A daily diagram had now been put in place comprising two return trips, at 07.45 and 11.55, from Crewe depot to Rhyl. Such running also acted as an additional shakedown operation and helped to identify a number of minor design issues that could be fed back into the construction cycle.

No D401 left Vulcan on 16 October and the next day made a trial trip to Carlisle, hauling 15 coaches. This was curtailed by the traction inspector at Blackburn,

because the radiator shutters were sticking open. A few other faults were also identified, and on the 18th No D401 went to Crewe Works for rectification. Next day a freight trial was cancelled due to lack of suitable rolling stock and a guard, the latter due to industrial action which then prevented further commissioning trips.

Curiously, BR decided to make first use of the 'D400s' on Crewe–Perth segments of through trains from Euston. Just why this was favoured over the (perhaps) more obvious services to Glasgow is not known. During early November No D401 was on the 1S05 22.50 ex Crewe, with Alan Chamberlain monitoring the locomotive. Part of his checks and observations included noting readings on voltmeter and ammeter equipment wired up to measure the main-generator output. He was concerned to find that the readings suggested a gross engine power of around 2,900-3,000bhp. In consequence No D401 was returned to Vulcan for investigation. Meanwhile Nos D402 and D403 had arrived at Crewe for commissioning, while No D400 remained active for training BR staff.

Vulcan eventually identified why No D401 was 'over-powering'. An engine governor operates in a band (range) when under full power. Normally, an increase in demand to

Newly delivered from Vulcan, No D403 awaits the start of commissioning at Crewe Works in November 1967.
EE

full power pushes the governor to the top of the band before it quickly settles back to the bottom of the band at a steady maximum output. This is the point on the band used when engines are set up on a load bank to produce the rated power. On the new class the control system caused the governor to be held at the top of the band whilst a train was accelerating. Hence during acceleration the engine was being asked by the governor to develop several hundred horsepower more than its rating. Correcting the quirk involved engines' being set up on a load bank with the governor in top-of-the-band state. The down side of setting up the engine in this way came when speed was falling during hill-climbing. In such situations the engine output would only be about 2,500bhp, even though the driver was demanding full power. This helps explain why drivers and observers have regarded a 'D400' as inferior to a 'D1500' or even a 'D11' on Shap, Beattock and on the Settle–Carlisle line.

No D403 proved a bit of a problem child due to difficulties with regulation of the ETH generator; these teething troubles resulted in its being put to one side at Crewe and accepted after No D404. Following commissioning, Nos D402 and D404 went to Polmadie and Perth respectively for staff training. This continued into January 1968 and involved return trips between Glasgow and Dumfries and between Perth and Stirling.

January 1968 saw the delivery rate from Vulcan increase, and by the end of the month Nos D400-6 had all been accepted, with Nos D407-9 following on 2 February.

Two trial runs – one on passenger and one on freight stock – were now required. Even though No D409 fluffed its freight trip on 18 January due to low power, BR waived a repeat run. Checks revealed serious oil contamination of the pressurising-fan motor in No D400, and this was deemed to be due to poor engine-room ventilation. In consequence, release of No D410 from Vulcan was delayed to enable baffles and doors to be fitted in the engine room to separate it into two compartments between the engine area and the generator area.

By the end of January Nos D400 and D405 were appearing at Perth on one of the overnight sleeper trains and, together with No D404, began to be used in rotation on driver training. Typically, during the day two return trips were made to Stirling, and the locomotive could then return to Crewe on the 22.35 ex Perth.

In early February No D406 went to Derby for evaluation by the BR Headquarters testing staff at the Railway Technical Centre. Although it was rigged up for full dress trials, these were cancelled due to cost. Instead a comparison was arranged with a Brush Type 4 on the recently closed Butterley branch, to assess wheelslip protection. The Western Region was prevailed upon to

Left: **No D403 experienced problems during commissioning but is seen here setting off from Crewe on a trial run in December 1967. Fortunately for BR, EE gave a 12 month warranty on all major components with each locomotive.** *EE*

Below: **Photographs of the class being commissioned are uncommon, so this view of No D435 on its northbound trip from Crewe to Carlisle on 30 July 1968 is worthy of inclusion. The train is seen passing Oxenholme.** *Derek Cross*

By April 1968 the delivery rate from Vulcan was around four locomotives per month. Nos D416/21/0/14 are seen undergoing commissioning on the 21st. *David Percival*

loan its dynamometer car, but the trials came to a premature end when the highly specialised coupling between this car and the locomotive became defective. The WR was not amused! No D406 was retained at Derby for tests of engine-room airflow until returned to Vulcan on 26 February for modifications.

Driver training at other LMR depots gradually progressed, starting with those along the WCML and broadening gradually to include those in the Liverpool, Manchester and Stoke divisions. This work proved useful for monitoring locomotives that had been reported in trouble. For example, on 8 February No D405 was failed at Bay Horse (between Preston and Lancaster) due to a traction-motor-blower problem; it was removed at Carnforth and taken to Crewe, where no fault was found. On the 9th it was sent to Lostock Hall shed for driver-training work. Around the same time No D400 was taken off its train at Carlisle, due to persistent wheelslip. No fault was found on depot, and it then worked a training turn before going overnight to Perth without incident.

One former EE commissioning engineer suggested drivers disliked the new diesels and would try to avoid taking one. To prove the point, he said a 'D400' could not obtain vacuum pressure at the head of a train at Crewe. Eventually he found that a train brake pipe had been uncoupled, but by then the 'D400' had been declared a failure and a replacement summoned. Driver unfamiliarity contributed to on-line failures. Site reports suggest the incident in question may have been on 13 March, when No D405 was failed by the driver due to an inability to take power whilst on the

07.58 'liner' at Crewe. The log states that no fault was found on examination and that the incident could only have happened due to reduction of pressure in a brake pipe. The failure was blamed on driver error.

On 21 February No D401 was on the 09.25 ex Crewe to Perth. At Motherwell the overload fault light came on and would not clear. The driver isolated all six traction motors, but still the fault light persisted. Assistance duly arrived, and this established that the driver had been using the wrong procedure to clear the fault. Now, though, No D401 would not take power, so it was declared a failure. The lack of power was due to the driver's forgetting he had isolated all the traction motors!

SHAKEDOWN ISSUES

The dynamic-brake equipment had become an issue by March, and agreement had been gained from BR to a trial whereby six examples would run with the equipment isolated. So that driver training with the dynamic brake in operation would not be prejudiced, Nos D420-5 (then unbuilt) were selected for the trial. A further issue was also emerging in the shape of KV10 lock-ons. The KV10 controls the main generator, and faulty circuitry caused it to lock in the full position, even with minimum power-controller opening; driving is then impossible. To this day, KV10 lock-ons are a not infrequent occurrence, and the only real solution is repair of the offending circuit board.

With increasing numbers in traffic and not needed for training, by the end of February the class was to be found on an expanding range of Anglo-Scottish passenger, freight and 'liner' traffic. For some time during late February and into March No D410 suffered fuel starvation. Drivers reported low power or loss of power, and a series of attempts was made to solve the matter. On 27 March No D410 was reported low on power on arrival in Glasgow and found to have air in the fuel system, which was cleared. Put on the 'Mid-Day Scot' back to Crewe, with EE's Alec Williamson (for some time the EE rep at Carlisle) riding, the locomotive suffered fuel starvation whilst climbing Beattock. Air was bled out of the system, but the problem recurred climbing Shap and again at Carnforth and Garstang; by now it was so acute that a Class 40 had to haul the train forward to Crewe. Eventually No D410 was sent for load-bank tests at Toton to identify the cause. In fact, this fault occurred frequently across the fleet and was traced eventually to poor sealing of joints in the fuel-supply pipework. March 1968 also brought the first incidents of cracked cylinder-head ports (one each on No D400, on the 10th, and No D401) – a portent of a major – and expensive – problem to come. On the 26th the modifications to No D410's engine-room airflow were deemed a failure; now the baffles were to be fully sealed up to prevent engine air from contaminating the generators.

An interesting trial run was made on 7 April between Edinburgh and Glasgow. It involved No D405 and was a high-speed demonstration to highlight the potential for push-pull operation between these cities. The class was fitted from new for push-pull operation, but Peter Meredith, one of the LMR's Derby-based engineers, recalls difficulty in getting the system to work, due to signal interference from other circuits in the wiring. Nevertheless, 100mph running was achieved for the first time over the route. The need to provide extra units (to enable the principal daytime Anglo-Scottish passenger trains to be double-headed from May 1970) put paid to any ambitions the Scottish Region may have had in rostering 'D400s' between Edinburgh and Glasgow. Embarrassingly, No D405 suffered five engine shutdowns during the trials, and some nifty (and slightly irregular) action was needed by Tommy Wrighton to avoid a failure.

Clearly the incidents mentioned above give only a small flavour of the teething troubles being experienced. Early April brought formal expression of

Initial duties were between Crewe and Perth. No D412 was caught at Oxenholme in September 1969 on the 11.20 Perth–Birmingham, which it would haul as far as Crewe.
David N. Clough collection

No D430 heads south from Lancaster, with the castle in view, on 11 July 1968 in charge of a Glasgow–Euston service.
Derek Cross

dissatisfaction from BR to EE over the availability figures. Surprisingly (by modern standards for designs dating from the 1960s), these figures were not at all bad – always at least 70% and often 90%. For the period from 20 January to 6 April, 52 incidents caused loss of availability, with control gear and brake equipment accounting for 30 and BR being responsible for nine.

EARLY OPERATION

On 1 May 1968 ex-LNER Class A3 Pacific locomotive No 4472 *Flying Scotsman* was to make a special non-stop run between London King's Cross and Edinburgh. The day before, perhaps as a spoiler, the West Coast train operators staged a six-hour trial run between Euston and Glasgow for which No D409 provided traction north of Crewe.

Although all the class was equipped with the pipework to allow full fitting of weight-transfer-compensation equipment, only No D417 was fully rigged. This equipment was blamed (in error) by BR staff for low-power faults experienced during its early period of operation, whereas fuel starvation (as with No D410) was the issue. The confusion was due to the weight-

transfer indicator light remaining on, whereas the system should have cut out as speed rose. Cut-out took place at the first field-weakening in the traction motors (around 27mph), but fuel starvation meant main-generator amps were so low that the divert did not take place. On 27 February 1969 No D417 was assigned to the 02.45 Carlisle–Manchester Red Bank. During the run into Carlisle part of the bellows support at No 1 end broke away and fell on the track; as it dragged along it ripped the bellows and was removed. All the equipment was eventually removed during the first overhaul at Crewe Works. The verdict was that the class was sufficiently surefooted not to need the added complication of weight-transfer equipment.

Fleet delivery reached the halfway mark on 13 May 1968 with the release of No D425 from Vulcan and No D424 being booked to make its second commissioning run. By now typically four or five machines per month were emerging from the EE works. BR was keen for the contracted availability guarantee to commence, whereby EE would be penalised if less than 84% of the fleet was available for service. The Board selected 8 May as the start date because that was when No D424 arrived from Vulcan (although not commissioned), the contractual date being when half the class was in service.

PROBLEMS, PROBLEMS

Drivers' industrial action during late June disrupted commissioning, and no 'D400s' ran in service on 30 June. After a long break, standard practice required the engine to be 'barred' (turned) over by hand to check for problems. Nos D406/8/13/21 all had water ingress into cylinders, due to cracked cylinder heads. The cracking problem was getting worse. As a precautionary measure, to prevent serious engine damage due to water in cylinders causing a serious hydraulic lock, engines were to be barred over by hand after being switched off for just a few hours. Heads cracked at the bridge piece between the inlet-valve ports, and this allowed engine-cooling water to seep in when the engine was shut down. The problem was not confined to the 'D400s' but occurred also on EE 'D200s' (Class 40) and 'D6700s' (Class 37), though very few cracks were reported among BR Type 1s and 2s or in Portugal.

By the end of July EE had told BR of the steps being taken to isolate and resolve matters. A modified Mk 2a head was supplied, but probably the main cause was a defective casting by the EE foundry that produced the heads. Ultimately the problem was resolved by switching to a new, Mk 3 head, which had been produced as part of the design-updating work being carried out by EE on the 16CSVT engine. Nevertheless, 108 heads were changed in 1968, 97 in 1969/70, and a further 17 to August 1971. These figures illustrate the scale of the problem and how it went away after introduction of the Mk 3 design. Sometimes heads were changed when found to be leaking. Eventually a campaign change arrangement was initiated. Under this both BR and Vulcan personnel worked overtime at weekends to swap all the heads on individual engines. In addition to these on-site changes, starting with No D405 on 22 July 1968, engines were exchanged for units fitted with new heads. Two spare engines had been ordered as part of the contract to provide a pool for overhaul. Initially, however, new 16CSVTs off the production line were commandeered for the swaps. This meant that two locomotives (Nos 442/9) each had

an engine from new that had already been used in another class member (Nos 405/4 respectively). Over the following year 31 locomotives received a replacement engine. Contrary to popular myth, no engines were written off due to irreparable damage during this period, because the LMR's records show that on 14 April 1970 there were two spare engines – one at Crewe and one at Vulcan.

Exhaust-manifold pipework was also working loose at joints and allowing gas to escape. The train vacuum brake was the source of a further recurring problem, caused by a particular valve (VA1) not functioning correctly. These brake defects often brought on-line delays or failures. Although on-line failures due to a lack of train heat were initially blamed on the locomotives, later examination invariably revealed the cause to be defective coaching stock.

AUGUST 1968 OPERATIONS

By the beginning of August 1968, with the final withdrawal of BR steam all but achieved, a wider spread of 'D400' activity was evident. For example, No D431 powered the Kendal–Kilburn parcels; another example was No D436, noted in charge of the 08.00 Northwich–Warrington Arpley freight on 15 October. By virtue of the increasing number of such reports in the official logs, clearly the class was undertaking a high proportion of non-passenger work, something that is not always appreciated.

No D434 makes a fine sight as it negotiates Lancaster Castle station on 31 July 1968 with the down 'Mid-Day Scot'. The water column was still in use at this time. *David Cross*

Proof that Perth made *ad hoc* use of the stabled locomotive off the overnight Euston–Inverness, prior to its return on the balancing up train, is provided by the following. On 16 May No D416 was used on the 08.14 Perth–Edinburgh, whilst on 7 and 13 June the 08.14 Inverness–Edinburgh produced Nos D425 and D406 respectively. On 22 July No D421 went from Perth to Grangemouth on a freight and then back to Perth, and Grangemouth saw many similar visits.

Industrial action affecting the route over Beattock saw the class traverse the Waverley Route. On 28 June No D416 worked the 12.05 Euston–Glasgow through Craigentinny. The dispute continued into July, with No D429 appearing on the 1st, No D418 on the 2nd and No D400 on the 3rd. No D400 also made the first appearance of the class on a scheduled service at Glasgow Queen Street, on 13 July, when it was rostered to work the 13.10 to Aberdeen. Reputedly, there was a summer diagram on 08.15FO Birmingham–Aberdeen, returning on the up Postal, although whether the 'D400' ventured north of Perth is unclear.

Meanwhile Anglo-Scottish 'liners' from Gushetfaulds (Glasgow) to Longsight, Garston and York Way (London) were all rostered for a single 'D400' on an 850-ton timing load and unassisted over Shap. Company 'liners', such as the Rootes Group Gosford Green–Linwood, had a new EE Type 4. No 445 found employment on the 01.44 Uddingston–Cliffe cement on 11 November and No 441 on the 24th on the return 02.30 train; these were taken to/from Millerhill Yard, Edinburgh. Next day No 417 powered the 16.05 St Rollox– Herbrandston oil tanks. Later in the year, No 444 was assigned to Eastfield, possibly for training purposes, demonstrating the wide sphere of use.

No 448's commissioning needs special mention. Although accepted by BR, the locomotive suffered persistent engine shutdowns. The erstwhile 'Lakes Express' from Euston to Windermere was a useful train to trial an engine with problems, because it was a short out-and-back run from Crewe. Although the timing between Preston and Lancaster was the fastest booked for any train, the load had been reduced at Preston. No 448 became a regular on this service, and on one run the driver got so frustrated at having to restart the power unit that he burst into tears! Matters reached a head around Christmas 1968, when BR threatened to return the

No D433 storms Shap in September 1969 with the down 'Royal Scot'. Note the clear exhaust.
David N. Clough collection

errant machine to 'commissioning' status for detailed investigation. Bearing in mind the control system employed first-generation electronics, the tests on No 448 revealed 'spikes' in the circuits that caused protection systems to cut in and cause engine shutdown unnecessarily.

Looking at the delivery dates for the last 10, it is clear that production at Vulcan slowed down. Previously this had been between four or five a month, but a two-week gap elapsed from No 448's leaving works until No 449 made its debut. The late Michael Harris, for some time Managing Editor of Ian Allan's magazine titles and a former EE employee, considered this was due to growing concern among Vulcan employees over their future. The halcyon days of mass production for BR were ending, and few overseas orders existed to replace them. Hence 1968 drew towards a close on a melancholy note for many at Newton-le-Willows. No 449's delivery was some five months behind the contract schedule, and it is reported that EE paid BR liquidated damages for the locomotives that were delivered late.

With all the fleet in traffic all principal passenger, mail, newspaper, parcels and freight movements, day and night, were so diagrammed, the LMR working its new acquisitions very hard to maximise the return on the lease payments.

1969

The first major mishap occurred, ironically, to No 400, on 18 May 1969. It was powering 1S18 22.15 Euston–Glasgow when it collided on Beattock Bank with 1S07 21.30 Euston–Inverness, with No 417 at the head. The latter had slipped to a stand and No 400 was allowed forward to assist in the rear. Having restarted, No 417 drew ahead but then stalled again. Regrettably No 400's driver did not see the tail lamp of the Inverness train and ploughed into the rear coach, dying in the process. No 400 suffered extensive damage to its No 1 cab and was sent next day to Crewe Works, but repair work was slow. In the meantime its bogies were taken for No 402 and its engine for No 420.

Many drivers failed their locomotives due to 'excessive wheelslip'. The class was

Pictures of a Class 50 and a working steam engine are rare. Here No D404 waits at Morecambe with a boat train for Euston while Standard '4MT' 4-6-0 No 75019 waits with an engineers' train. *David Cross*

The 'Lakes Express', from Euston to Windermere, brought a Class 50 down the branch from Oxenholme, as also did the Kendal–Willesden vans. No D419 crosses the old River Lune bridge at Lancaster on 10 July 1968. *Derek Cross*

at least as good as the comparable Brush Type 4, neither being fitted with sanding gear, but the EE product had more rapidly acting electronic protection, as well as the current-limiting potentiometer – the so-called tractive-effort control. Enquiries of those involved at the time suggest there was wide variation among drivers in the use of the latter facility, which allowed the maximum traction current to be set at any value below full by turning a knob on the driver's dashboard. In poor rail conditions, when normal full power could not be sustained, the driver could use the control to set a lower current which represented a tractive effort capable of being sustained without wheelslip. Reputedly, Crewe drivers made virtually no use of this facility. In contrast, Longsight drivers used the tractive-effort control to start the heavy 'liner' to Glasgow. Bearing in mind the driver's power handle is a relatively crude means of power control, when compared to the tractive-effort control, Longsight men found the following technique worked best. With the locomotive put into 'forward', the tractive-effort control was wound right back to zero; the power handle was then opened to 'full', but no current passed to the traction motors until the tractive-effort control was slowly wound up by the driver. By slowly winding up the power in this way, wheelslip was avoided, and the best possible rate of acceleration achieved.

Alec Williams considers that good drivers used the tractive-effort control,

when conditions demanded it. In contrast, some drivers just opened the power handle to 'full' and expected the control system to take care of things, even if the traction motors were screaming in uncontrolled wheelslip. It thus becomes easy to see why engineers often say the biggest cause of locomotive failure is bad drivers!

EE provided a driver's handbook. At starting, 2,000-2,500A could be taken for 3sec before the locomotive moved and for 2-3min when on the move. Once speed had reached about 5mph, the power handle was to be opened fully. This driving style was not customary, however. On the footplate leaving Crewe one day, Alan Chamberlain was so frustrated watching the driver 'fidgeting' with the power controller that he leaned over and pulled it to 'full', and the train stormed away. At Preston an EE colleague came to the cab and said he had never departed Crewe so fast and he had come to check if there were two locomotives up front! Allan C. Baker – recently (2002) retired as Director of Engineering at Angel Trains – spent several years at Crewe depot when the '50s' were there. He confirms that a good single 'D400', on a comparable load, could match an electric for acceleration up to 70mph.

Alec Williams remembers having to deal with a curious low-power problem on No 444. This had been failed due to fuel starvation, and tests showed there was indeed a vacuum in the fuel-supply system. Further investigation proved inconclusive, and eventually a periscope was placed inside the fuel tank. With the aid of a torch, an empty bread wrapper was spotted, which must have been present since construction. All efforts to remove it failed, and the only solution was for Crewe to cut a hole in the tank and remove the wrapper by hand. The locomotive bears the tell-tale patch on its fuel tank to this day.

Selecting a week at random (w/e 30 August 1969) and examining the reports from the EE technicians at Crewe, Carlisle and Glasgow will offer an excellent picture of everyday life for the '400s'. Mr F. Holloway at Crewe had three failures to report. On the 26th No 448 was on the 22.15 Euston–Glasgow Central but was replaced at Wigan due to 'earth fault light'. Springs Branch depot found all six traction motors had the wrong grade of brushes fitted, and it took a week for replacements to arrive from Crewe! On the 29th No 407 was hauling the 23.15 Freightliner from York Way to Gushetfaulds but had to be removed at Winsford because of various difficulties. These transpired to be down to errors by Crewe depot staff in setting up the dynamic-brake gear. That evening the 19.27 Gosford Green–Linwood company train was delayed for 54 minutes at Wigan when No 425 suffered traction overloads. This was being monitored by depot staff after several similar reports, and the final outcome is not known.

In addition to these failures, No 432, with engine No IH6962, had all cylinder heads replaced with the Mk 3 pattern at Vulcan. No 447, with engine IH6848, was reported 'low power'. A load-bank test showed generator output of 1,648kW, and the governor was adjusted so that 1,798kW was produced. (Note: the theoretical generator output is given as 1,746kW at 2,700bhp engine output.) The opinion was that someone had been tampering with the governor linkage.

At Carlisle, Alec Williams reported seven failures. On 24 August No 413, in charge of the 23.55 Glasgow Central–Liverpool Exchange, was removed at Carlisle with a 'train-heat defect', costing six minutes. The cause was a failed interlock. Two days later No 434 was on the 22.30 Euston–Perth when the diesel shut down at Shap Wells and would not restart. Two days later the same thing happened in the same place whilst the locomotive was on the 12.05 Euston–Glasgow. Another two days later, with No 434 on the 13.15 Carlisle–Preston, the incident occurred

once more, this time at Howe & Co's sidings on the Settle–Carlisle line. Tests on depot failed to find the cause, and monitoring equipment was rigged up to isolate the fault, but local running on the 31st and a trial on the 08.30 Carlisle–Crewe on 1 September also drew a blank. On 3 September, on the 22.15 from Euston, No 434 shut down at Scout Green. (Note that two of the earlier failures had also been on Shap.) Now it was possible to isolate the problem, which turned out to be a defective voltage regulator which was failing to supply field excitation to the auxiliary generator.

On 25 August, meanwhile, No 423 was in trouble heading the 09.00 Manchester Victoria–Glasgow Central, being removed at Carlisle due to 'low power', the cause being a seized turbocharger. The 30th brought two incidents. Firstly No 412 was removed from the 23.20 Birmingham New Street–Glasgow Central at Carlisle with 'low power', but depot examination and a trial run found no fault. Later No 407 caused a 20min delay to the 12.05 Euston–Perth when it had to be removed at Carlisle due to 'overloads in notch 1', caused by a loose wire in the CU1 board.

North of the Border, on the 25th the automatic voltage relay on No 449 failed, causing a 70min delay to the 18.07 Gushetfaulds–Garston Freightliner at Garriongill. Next day No 429 expired at

No D447 calls at a quiet-looking Kendal with the up 'Lakes Express', the 16.15 ex Windermere on 9 September 1969.
David N. Clough collection

Elvanfoot on the 00.55 Liverpool Exchange–Glasgow Central, due to coolant draincocks' being left open. Next day the same locomotive was on the 07.20 Glasgow Central–Euston when the engine stopped, but no fault light lit up, and no fault could be found on depot. On the 28th No 429 suffered an identical shutdown at the head of the 22.15 Euston–Glasgow Central, and, after assistance to Carstairs, the diesel restarted. Nothing of substance was found, but the HOVR was reset to a higher voltage, as it was tripping out when the diesel engine surged and thus caused shutdown.

Looking at accumulated miles and engine hours reveals quite varying overall average speeds. For example, in 14 months No 429 had run 128,390 miles in 6,014 engine hours – 21.3 miles per engine hour (mpeh) or 110,049 miles per annum. No 449 had run 75,930 miles in 3,617 engine hours – 21mpeh, 107,195 miles per annum. Contrast these with No 418 at the end of June, with 128,780 miles at an average of 26.3mpeh or 110,383 miles per annum. These annual mileages were very high, demonstrating the intensity of use. The relatively low average speed shows the mixed-traffic nature of the work performed, though some examples had averaged over 30mpeh.

A sample of 'lesser' freight turns assigned to the class is illustrated by use on the Liverpool Brunswick–Ordsall Lane tanks and Ford's Halewood–Wakefield, whilst penetration into the West Midlands is demonstrated by No 403 taking the 06.00 Manchester Red Bank to Walsall vans on 19 May 1969. In fact, appearances in Birmingham had begun in 1968, when the class visited Tyseley for tyre turning. Usually a train would be hauled to New Street as part of the journey. Tyre turning also involved visits to Willesden. By now BR had contracted for the TOPS system of rolling-stock tracking and control, under which the 'D400s' became Class 50.

Merseyside Railway Society (MRS) members' observations in the North West have also added to the information about this period. On 6 June David Rapson spent a few hours on the Settle–Carlisle line, observing No 409 heading north with a special tank train 6Z37; at this time the Herbrandston–Sighthill (St Rollox) tanks was booked for a Class 50, so this may have been an out-of-course working. Later No 448 passed on 7A09 Carlisle Yard–Willesden (load 50), No 417 had charge of the 7P45 Crewe Basford Hall–Carlisle Yard, and finally No 447 passed with the 7M49 02.00 Margam–Carlisle Yard (load 51).

Lunchtime observations at Liverpool Exchange by MRS member Alan Turton offer an interesting insight into how some of the technical troubles that blighted the period up to late 1969 served to reduce availability. As expected, train 1M27 – the 08.20 from Glasgow and Edinburgh – produced a 'D400' virtually daily by July 1968 after a first visit on 1 June. After fuelling at Edge Hill, the locomotive would take the northbound service at 17.45. From 9 October 1968, however, hardly a single Class 50 put in an appearance until mid-February 1969, and it was to be a further month before the new diesels fully held sway again.

MRS observations at Moore, just south of Warrington (and a point where the WCML and Chester lines diverge) exemplify the availability difficulties. The longest stint was from 08.00 to 16.00 on 13 August 1969. Half the fleet was noted – very good, when one takes account of those locomotives performing duties entirely north of Warrington. This supports Peter Meredith's assertion that the Operating Department called on him to provide 90% availability on summer Saturdays. On two other days during August, over a period of about an hour less, 12 and 16 locomotives were observed – not so good.

Interestingly, on all three days several WCML expresses had Brush Type 4s; only

Ever in action, No D435 shoots through the Lune Gorge at Tebay with the up 'Royal Scot'.
D. E. Canning

seven passenger, parcels or freight trains had a Class 50 on all three days, and two of those were from Blackpool South to Euston. The 09.30 Perth–Euston produced tandem traction on two days, with a Brush/EE pairing on the 13th and Nos 416 and 437 on the 30th. Proving the class had at least one daily diagram from Manchester Victoria to North Wales, on the 13th No 432 headed the 11.40 Llandudno–Manchester. Other reports have confirmed this as not an isolated occurrence. Finally, despite pressure on motive power at the height of the summer, a good crop of freights had a Class 50 up front.

FURTHER PROBLEMS

The unexpected cost and loss of availability due to cylinder-head failures was just about easing when a fresh engine

defect emerged. Excessive oil scraping within the cylinders caused piston seizures and serious damage; typically, the connecting rod would then break free from the seized piston and smash around wildly, usually bursting a hole in the crankcase. The balance between too much and too little oil scraping by the scraper rings fitted to each piston is a very fine one. The first failure was suffered by No 410 on 13 August at Blainscough with the 19.02 Longsight–Glasgow 'liner', when A5 piston seized and the connecting rod came through the side of engine IH6937. Engine IH6964 had been removed from No 436 at Vulcan and stripped for crankshaft examination. Having been rebuilt, it was sent to Crewe Works for load-bank running-in, after being installed in No 410. Some time during the early 1970s engine

Above left: **No D418 is seen near Crawford with a Manchester–Glasgow train on 24 March 1970, by which time it had acquired multiple-working equipment on its cab fronts in readiness for the May 1970 timetable.** *Derek Cross*

Above: **One of No 400's inertial filters, showing the build-up of dirt, recorded on 11 March 1969.** *BR*

Very rare track for Class 50 – the far end of the Bootle branch. With dented cab front, No D439 (officially 439) was given the responsibility of taking the 'Tote Investors' Special' from Euston to Aintree Racecourse station for the Grand National meeting on 4 April 1970. Aintree engine shed is on the left. *David Rapson*

IH6941 was written off, seemingly due to a similar failure. No 410 was by no means the only casualty, and, to reduce the instances of excessive oil scraping, sanction was given to remove the bottom scraper ring. Engine IH6945 in No 415 was the first to be dealt with, in August 1970, and IH6954 in No 433 was the last, on 10 June 1971. EE provided two technicians at Crewe depot to do the work, with Crewe Works also doing some.

During No 400's first 'E' examination, in March 1969, by which time it had completed 4,709 running hours, the build-up of dirt on the inertial filters caused comment. The units were sent to Crewe Works for cleaning, but pressure-washing had no effect. A proprietary chemical solvent bath had to be used for four hours. By July, when comparative checks were made on the cleanliness of electrical machines across different EE diesel types, matters had deteriorated; despite being the newest, the '400s' had the worst dirt and oil contamination. Depot standards were noted as a factor, Haymarket being identified as very good. Modifications to No 414's ventilation system had made matters worse.

To cap all this, concern was growing about locomotive interior air-management arrangements. These had been voiced even before No 400 had left Vulcan and grew steadily, but consideration of these issues will be deferred to the next chapter.

Eventually a major design fault was diagnosed: the intake grilles for the inertial filters were at roof level, meaning that the air drawn in came straight from the engine exhaust ports and was thus hardly clean. Of course, this was not the sort of material that the inertial filters were designed to cope with, and they didn't.

As if this were not enough, 1969 brought the first main-generator flashovers. To be fair, by no means all were the generator's fault. No 449 suffered the first, on 13 March, whilst on the Carlisle–Manchester Red Bank empty vans. A loose connection on No 4 traction motor caused the generator to flash over, and EE staff effected a repair at Crewe depot. Depot staff usually managed to deal with flashovers, but sometimes these were so serious as to require Crewe Works or EE to do the work. There were four causes of failures. Sometimes the main generator would flash over in sympathy with a traction motor and was not at fault (as on No 449 above). Sometimes the flashover was due to oil or coolant getting into the windings – again, not the machine's fault. It was, however, the highest-rated DC main generator used in BR service and pushed technology to its limit; in subsequent locomotive designs AC power generators were used. Finally, the LMR considered that materials used in construction (notably the mica used for insulation) were not the best.

It had not been the start EE and the LMR had wanted. Equipment – engine and generator – trialled in DP2 had given unexpected trouble. Whilst there were problems with the electronics, these could have been expected from a full-blown roll-out of first-generation technology. On-line difficulties did not endear the class to drivers, but a significant proportion of failures were caused by driver error, such as not resetting overload or overspeed cut-outs or ensuring fuel, oil and water supplies were sufficient before leaving the depot. It is clear that the 84% availability guarantee was only being met infrequently. When operational, a locomotive was allowed to rest for barely an hour, day and night, before the LMR deployed it on its next duty. Passenger schedules north of Crewe could now be timed on the use of a 2,700bhp traction unit, rather than most having to be allocated to a 2,000bhp EE Type 4 – progress, but with no small amount of pain.

4

Double-heading and Downgrading

EARLY RUNNING EXPERIENCE

From 4 May 1970 the LMR and ScR revamped the WCML Anglo-Scottish timetable. The objective was a speeding-up of the principal services and a rationalisation generally. Before looking at these changes, however, a review of train running by the class in the first couple of years in traffic is needed; this will help to set the scene for the 1970 developments.

O. S. Nock described a run in *Railway Magazine* in December 1969, featuring No 409 hauling 13 cars for 495 tons gross. Departing Preston 6½min late, the train attained an excellent 91mph before Lancaster, passed in 18min 25sec. Thereafter 87mph was achieved twice, at Carnforth and Milnthorpe. Grayrigg and Shap summits were breasted at 50.5mph and 41mph respectively, with a time to the latter of 52min 40sec for the 58.7 miles. Down to Carlisle three slowings for track work marred progress. Accelerating across the near-level length between Preston and Lancaster, and between Carnforth and Milnthorpe, the engine output works out at around 2,780bhp, whilst on the upper part of Grayrigg it was 2,560bhp. Although no date is given for the run, it is assumed no train heat was being supplied. Demonstrating that this was no isolated incident, the same year Michael Oakley timed No 424 with a similar load on a service that called at Oxenholme. Having restarted from there, it stormed Grayrigg at 49mph and topped Shap at 41mph, as with No 409 on the previous run. The power output from Oxenholme, when No 424 was accelerating, was again 2,780bhp, while the effect of the 1-in-75 climb to Shap, with speed falling against the grade, meant No 424's output dropped similarly to 2,560bhp. These early experiences by recorders confirmed Alan Chamberlain's findings with No D401 during initial testing, that the control system demanded peak engine output only during acceleration, when the governor was held at the top of the band of its range.

Comparison with a Class 47 effort on a 465-ton consist, timed by Mr Nock in 1966 and published by Ian Allan Ltd in *Sixty Years of West Coast Express Running*, gives the honours to Class 50; despite the heavier load, as far as Oxenholme. The Class 47, however, had the better of it up Grayrigg. Whether No 1861 had been derated from 2,750 to 2,580bhp by then is not known, but it managed no more than 88mph before Lancaster, by which point it was 30sec slower than No 409. Passing Carnforth at 85mph, No 1861 had fallen to 69 by Oxenholme, but the minimum at Grayrigg was a remarkable 58mph – easily the best climb published with a Class 47. The following table compares salient elements of the runs with the two types.

	Barton to Bay Horse	Carnforth to Oxenholme	Oxenholme to Grayrigg
	Time (min/sec)	Time (min/sec)	Time (min/sec)
No 409 (495 tons)	7.34	9.50	7.15
No 1861 (465 tons)	7.57	9.50	6.43
	Rail hp	Rail hp	Rail hp
No 409	2,175	2,085	1,960
No 1861	1,800	2,070	2,185

The climbs to Grayrigg, Shap and Beattock invariably were from high speed at the bottom, with a gradual deceleration against the grade. It is not surprising, therefore, that drivers and recorders alike looked upon the better minima produced by the Brush locomotive as a sign that it was superior. This, of course, was only part of the story, because in getting up to speed and sustaining high speed the EE type had a definite edge.

Note that both Nos 409 and 424 were producing 2,780bhp – slightly above the 2,650-2,750bhp range stipulated as usual by the manufacturer. This does not signify calculation error, and the following will serve to indicate that excessive power was not uncommon. Crewe depot had a load bank installed to enable engine testing and running-in to be carried out there. This allowed concerns about – say – driver reports of low power or engine surging to be verified on the depot by precise measurement of engine power. During the second half of 1969 several locomotives were monitored in this way, and some interesting results emerged. On 6 August No 441 was wired up. With the engine and generator cold, 2,065kW was developed, dropping to 2,010kW when hot; 1,746kW is the 'book' rating for the main generator. These generator outputs correspond to 3,190 engine bhp, against the 2,700bhp normal rating.

What had caused the over-powering is unknown, but it must have been incorrect adjustment of something by maintenance staff. It demonstrates that Class 50 was capable of abnormally high outputs, as measured by observers in the train, and debunks those who blame recorder error for such performances. No 441 was reset to normal output, after which a check revealed the load-bank instrumentation to be incorrectly calibrated! Now No 441 was shown as producing 1,630kW, rather than 1,760kW as thought, so it was reset again to an accurate normal power level. This

under-recording does, of course, mean that the true output when first tested was around 2,160kW, or over 3,300 engine bhp! Other examples of excessive power detected on the load bank at this time include No 440 recorded at 1,920kW and No 446 at 1,840kW; the latter was tested at an output of 2,060kW – nearly 3,200bhp.

DOUBLE-HEADING

The running described above represented the pinnacle of single Type 4 performance with prevailing speed limits and a 455-ton timing load. Although first-class, the efforts by Nos 409 and 424 were neither isolated nor unusual during 1968 and 1969. In fact, such data as is available suggests that this was a typical standard. Clearly the margin of Class 50 over Class 47, especially when power had to be sacrificed by the former for train heating (rather than traction) during colder months, was small. At the time very few of the latter class had an ETH capability.

Schedule time from Preston to Carlisle on No 1861's run was 94min, but this had stretched to 97.5min by 1968 to accommodate track relaying with continuous welded rail. This gives average

A new era was ushered in on the WCML on 5 May 1970, with pairs of '50s' working the principal daytime passenger services. The down 'Royal Scot' was provided specially with a headboard. Clean Nos D437 and D447 back onto the train at Crewe. *BR*

Above: The corresponding up working on 5 May did not carry a headboard. Nos D430 and D409 nevertheless make a fine sight passing Lamington, in the Clyde Valley. *Derek Cross*

Left: A superb array of signals outside Carstairs frames Nos 421 and 402 on train 1M26, a Perth-Euston service, on 25 April 1970. *Derek Cross*

speeds for the 90.1 miles of 57.5 and 55.5mph respectively. Net times for Nos 409 and 1861 were around 79min, at 68.4mph average. Between Carlisle and Glasgow timings were even more leisurely.

Whilst times such as those achieved by Nos 409 and 1861 could not be scheduled, because of the need to allow recovery time for delays and variability between locomotives, clearly there was scope for time-saving, even with a single Type 4. In May 1968 Cecil J. Allen timed a Class 50 on the up 'Royal Scot' from Carlisle. With a 425-ton load, No D415 arrived in Crewe in 126min net for 141.1 miles – an average of 67.2mph. This represented a gain on the net schedule (after deducting 18min recovery time) of 12½min. During this journey the time from Carlisle to Shap Summit (31min 20sec) represented an average speed of over 60mph. It was not the fastest southbound ascent recorded, for Michael Oakley noted better with a similar 11-coach load.

April 1969 brought a Government announcement that £30.4 million was to be spent on track rationalisation and re-signalling work between Weaver Junction (where the electrified line to Liverpool diverges from the WCML) to Glasgow. The work was planned to take until 1973 and would remove the blanket limit of 75mph north of Gretna Junction. On completion, the London–Glasgow journey was expected to take five hours, in comparison with 6¾ hours at the time. It was a further year before the Government committed itself to electrifying the whole route, and meanwhile matters had been put in hand for a general speeding-up.

If overall timings were to be reduced radically, either loads would have to be cut or more power provided. Given that the type was built with a multiple-working facility, the solution chosen was to deploy two Class 50s on the principal daytime Anglo-Scottish expresses from the Summer 1970 timetable. To facilitate this, all the class had full multiple-unit fittings added during early 1970; as built, only No 400 had been so fitted, whilst No 401 had external connection ports.

The new timetable brought quite a radical change and was really the first to take advantage not only of locomotives working in multiple but also of the general use of large Type 4s of around 2,700bhp north of Weaver Junction. It was recast to provide five daytime London–Glasgow

services, all of which had limited stops south of Preston. All five trains, together with the 08.15 from Birmingham and 08.15 from Liverpool (with through carriages from Manchester attached at Preston), had two Class 50s working in multiple. In the up direction, all the Londons were double-headed, as too were the evening return workings to Liverpool and Birmingham. Downgrading of the Liverpool Exchange–Preston route brought a switch to Liverpool Lime Street, enabling St Helens and Wigan to be served.

The down 'Royal Scot' was now booked for 6½min under six hours – an average of 68.1mph and inclusive of stops at Crewe and Carlisle. Completion of the first phase of West Coast electrification to the North West had allowed the down 'Royal Scot' to be timed from Euston in 121min to Crewe, with a 149min booking to Carlisle. By 1968 the latter section was timed at 157min, with no less than 18min recovery allowance; from 4 May 1970 this was slashed to just 8min. Bearing in mind that No D415 above had gained 12min between Carlisle and Crewe, there was also clearly some potential to slim down the basic timings, even with a single Class 50. Added to this, from May 1970 some speed limits north of Weaver Junction were eased, and four lengths – Weaver Junction–Acton Grange Junction, Burton–Milnthorpe, Plumpton–Southwaite and north from Carlisle to the Border – were cleared for 100mph. Set against this background, the seemingly spectacular 53min speed-up for the 'Royal Scot' (to take one example) by virtue of twin '50' power north of Crewe can be put in context. In short, probably 30min could have been saved even with a single locomotive.

On 10 March 1970 Nos 443 and 416 took part in a trial run to test the new schedules, whereby an 11-coach special (375 tons) ran from Crewe to Glasgow. G. J. Aston timed the trip for *Modern Railways*. The special was allowed a net time of 112½min from Crewe to Carlisle (75.3mph average) but managed 109min net. Between Carlisle and Glasgow the special was allowed 87min net, whereas the 'Royal Scot' was scheduled for a gross time of 98min. Nos 443 and 416 only managed a net run of 89½min, proving that the schedule, requiring a 70.6mph average, was too tight for the prevailing 75mph ceiling in Scotland.

Naturally the uphill running was virtually unparalleled. Speed rose from 79.5mph at Oxenholme to 82 at Lambrigg, before an easing to 71 through Grayrigg. Shap Summit had a 60mph restriction, and this precluded an all-out effort up the bank. Beattock Bank, of course, was subject to the overall 75mph ceiling, but even so Nos 443 and 416 were driven hard, with 77.5mph at the bottom and 64.5mph at the top. Analysing these performances indicates a combined 4,040rhp – 5,400bhp after allowing for train heat.

In the up direction from Glasgow, the pair managed a net time of 84$\frac{1}{2}$min (86$\frac{1}{2}$ booked), but only by dint of an 82mph average between Beattock Summit and Gretna Junction. From Carlisle to Preston the 73min booking was cut to 67$\frac{1}{2}$min net, although there was less gain thereafter to Crewe. Here 41min was allowed, and this was cut by only one minute. The foregoing, by a pair of locomotives producing rated output, shows far tighter timing against the motive power's capabilities than in previous years. Bear in mind also that the drivers ran as hard as the Civil Engineer allowed, and these trial runs represented the best that was practical without raising these speed limits.

The May 1970 timetable required eight pairs of Class 50s for the 14 trains (seven each way). Accordingly, an extra eight locomotives (16% of the fleet) had to be released from other duties, mainly daytime freights. Although the actual diagramming is not available, it seems likely that the authorities would have rostered an availability of 84%, the figure guaranteed by EE, particularly as the early engine problems were settling down.

Cecil J. Allen travelled on the inaugural down 'Royal Scot', made up to 13 coaches, 460 tons gross – the timing maximum. Nos 437 and 447 would have had a riding fitter and probably also a traction inspector accompanying the footplate crew to ensure matters went to plan. Winsford Junction was passed at 100mph in 8min 3sec – a minute to the good. However, a permanent-way slack (pws) after Weaver Junction cost about 2$\frac{1}{2}$min, and little had been recovered before an almost inevitable signal check approaching Euxton Junction and a further pws before Preston. Despite 4min recovery time, the latter was passed 2min 15sec down, in 47min 45sec.

A steady 95mph (instead of the permitted 90) onwards to Lancaster pulled back a minute. Milnthorpe saw a second 100mph for the trip, and Oxenholme was passed at 82. Grayrigg was topped at 72. Acceleration to 92mph through Tebay and 68mph minimum (60 permitted) over Shap Summit meant the train was now over a minute early, and fast running down to Carlisle, including 100mph from Plumpton to Southwaite, brought a Carlisle arrival in 107.5min net – slightly faster than the trial run – 5.5min having been gained by the pair on the net schedule. The 31.4 miles from Carnforth to Shap Summit had been reeled off at an average of 84.7mph. In contrast, the same distance down to Carlisle was covered at an average of 78.4. Such was the benefit of the extra tractive effort in 'flattening' the hills.

Mr Allen did not provide tabular detail north of the Border. Beattock was topped at 60mph, but a succession of delays saw Glasgow reached 14.5min behind time. Perhaps unsurprisingly, Nos 437 and 447 were delivering around 4,140rhp, suggesting a normal maximum effort. Although other trips around this period were of a similar standard, as the 1970s progressed, so considerable variation crept into performances. Nevertheless, drivers sometimes put in some lively efforts, with maxima of 106mph reported, generally between Crewe and Weaver Junction and between Preston and Lancaster.

The Operating Department introduced a special bell code for signalling the trains that ran to the accelerated timings and were booked for two Class 50s; the code was 4-4-6. A special code of 2-2-2 had also to be given to signify 'train entering section'. The objective was to minimise the risk of delaying these double-headed trains, because dozy signalmen were slow in pulling off their signals for a fast-approaching train. Studying logs of runs during this period reveals that the incidence of signal checks remained quite high, although this may have been due to prevailing traffic levels.

Sometimes the rostered pair was not available, and a run timed by a Mr Murton on the 13.45 Glasgow–Euston demonstrated what a single machine could achieve. No 425 had 390 tons but reached Preston in 75min 13sec. This was 2min ahead of schedule, although deducting 6min recovery time from the latter reveals

Right: **For a couple of years after May 1971 the former G&SW route was used to permit electrification of the railway over Beattock. On 30 July 1971 Nos 445 and 424 thread their way past Kilmarnock with the up 'Royal Scot'.** *Derek Cross*

Far right: **Sometimes it was necessary to divert trains even further west from Kilmarnock. On 23 July 1973 No 439 threads Dalry Junction, north of Ayr, with train 1S69 (12.15 Euston–Glasgow), which ran as a relief to the 12.05 service and was booked for just a single Class 50.** *Derek Cross*

a loss of 4min on the net schedule, albeit still excellent with only half the rostered power.

AVAILABILITY, RELIABILITY AND TIMEKEEPING

Some have suggested that the use of two locomotives was to ensure the train reached its destination, due to the likely prospect of one failing! Designating the fleet as Class 50, it was said, was because one had only a 50% chance of getting there on time! Others have remarked that availability was so poor that many

Class	Availability %	Miles per year	Miles per casualty	Cost per mile (pence)
55	75	144,000	14,000	28
52	75	105,000	15,000	24
50	70	106,000	9,000	15
47	78	72,000	12,000	19
45	77	71,000	11,000	21

services failed to be provided with the booked two machines.

Looking at logs timed by enthusiasts reveals how prone the running was to disruption and delay. Not wishing to carry the can, the Operating Department blamed the locomotives for late running, whilst the engineers blamed the Operating Department.

Timekeeping was not helped by the onset of electrification work in May 1971, and liberal amounts of recovery time reappeared in the schedules. In addition, most daytime trains were routed via the Glasgow & South Western to enable the Caledonian line to be given over to the Civil Engineer. Arguments over punctuality came to a head in 1973, when all the class was ridden for a fortnight to establish the cause of poor timekeeping. Peter Meredith states that on only one occasion was the blame laid at the door of the '50s'. Availability was not good, however, as official figures for 1971 (left) show:

Left: The Settle–Carlisle line has long been a regular diversionary option when the WCML is out of commission. Sunday diversions on 12 September 1971 saw a pair of '50s' crossing Ribblehead Viaduct with a train for Glasgow.
David N. Clough collection

Below: On 5 February 1973 another electrification diversion – albeit extremely short – brought the up 'Royal Scot' onto the Liverpool–Manchester Victoria line at Parkside. Nos 407 and 425 had left the WCML at Golborne Junction and would pass Vulcan before regaining the normal route at Winwick Junction.
David N. Clough

Whilst based on the LMR, the Class 50s were allocated to Crewe Diesel Depot. On 3 April 1971 No 411 receives repairs that involve a bogie lift. *David H. Allen*

The low cost per mile for Class 50 reflects that only light overhauls were carried out. As time in service lengthened, and intermediate overhauls began, so the cost per mile rose, and for 1972 it was 16p. Between 1 January 1972 and 18 May 1973 an average of seven machines (14%) were stopped at Crewe depot for scheduled maintenance with, typically, another 10 (20%) out of service on depots or Crewe Works for unplanned reasons. Clearly 84% was not being attained. Neville Davies, then Depot Engineer at Crewe, reports that the diagrammed availability was reduced to 70% when it became obvious that 84% was unattainable.

Of note also was the rise in miles per engine hour (mpeh). Whereas in Chapter 3 this was seen to be typically 21-22mpeh during the first couple of years, by 1971, with greater deployment on passenger rosters, the average was 37.5mpeh. The year proved a milestone in terms of mileages, because thereafter there was a gradual fall-off. Average mileages per annum were as set out in the table above, although that for 1974 was a projected figure, and by that year average speed per engine hour was down to 25.

Year	Miles
1968	95,000
1969	102,000
1970	103,000
1971	106,000
1972	99,000
1973	89,000
1974	78,000

The lower average mileages per annum are explained partly by the continuing fall in availability. Locomotives standing idle awaiting attention are not clocking up miles, and the more there are in this state the lower will be the overall class mileage, and therefore the overall average per locomotive drops. Mr Davies says that cost constraints meant that Crewe depot had insufficient artisan staff to deal with the level of maintenance required for Class 50. This meant that locomotives could stand idle on depot awaiting their turn for routine examinations or unscheduled repairs. Poor availability of spare parts, both from Crewe Works and from EE, also caused locomotives to stand idle. Robbing one machine to return another to traffic was common, but this effectively doubled work and involved disturbing electronic components which frequently then caused on-line failures. In the light of experience this practice was abandoned at the depot, but it continued at Crewe Works. The argument that expensive locomotives were standing idle for want of additional depot manpower cut no ice with higher authority and this was reflected in the LMR's acceptance that 70% availability was the best it could achieve with its fleet whilst working the punishing high-speed, high-mileage diagrams. Unfortunately official records on rostering are not available, but an

Above: **Other depots carried out running repairs and 'A' exams but not scheduled maintenance. Among these was Springs Branch, Wigan, where No 429 is seen stabled outside the former steam shed in 1972.**
David N. Clough

Left: **Until December 1976 Crewe Works handled overhauls. No 50002 is seen undergoing a light classified overhaul on 20 September 1975.**
David N. Clough

interesting indication of how many trains had the booked two engines can be gained from the following table, compiled from timings made by Dave Coddington.

Clearly most of the trains had their booked two locomotives. Some of the journeys where only a single Class 50 was diagrammed were on overnight services. The failure rate was certainly higher than the official figures, but one run classed here as a failure was where the engine was changed at Carlisle after time was lost

	1970	*1971*	*1972*	*Three-year total*
Runs each year	28	22	24	74
Miles	3,183	3,132	2,909	9,224
Booked for pair	24	21	22	67
Pair allocated	22 (92%)	17 (81%)	21 (95%)	60 (90%)
Booked single	4	2	2	8
Actual single	3	1	2	6
Failure	1		1	2
Miles per casualty				4,612

en route, and this may not have been due to motive-power problems.

Mr Davies comments that maintenance planning was still in its infancy. Depot staff tended to be conservative in providing the Operating Department with expected release times for locomotives. In turn, the latter distrusted their maintenance colleagues and also built in a further contingency margin. The result could be that only a single locomotive was rostered instead of a pair, despite a second machine actually being available.

From 6 June 1973 BR began to renumber its entire fleet of locomotives to denote the classification that had been devised in 1968. No 426 was the first, becoming No 50026 on 29 July 1973, and No 413 was the last, adopting its new identity of 50013 on 19 June 1974. The majority of the renumbering took place in the first four months of 1974, and this was done at Crewe depot.

TECHNICAL ISSUES

Several technical issues now need to be covered, because these impacted on both availability and reliability. First, picking up on the piston-seizure problems discussed in Chapter 3, BR was so concerned that it carried out tests on two locomotives during the summer of 1970. The purpose was to establish whether piston-crown cracking was related to the seizures and whether abnormally high cylinder temperatures were a factor. Whilst the technicalities of the report go beyond the scope of this book, the findings are most illuminating.

On separate days during July and August Nos 409 and 413 respectively were fully instrumented and put on the 08.15 Birmingham–Glasgow and return as part of a pair, the instrumented locomotive being in the lead going north. On both days that tests were carried out the load was given as 455 tons. On each occasion the engineer found obtaining readings at full

A snowy scene near Shap Summit on 3 February 1974, with Nos 50027 and 429 on the up 'Royal Scot'. No 50027 had been renumbered a month before, whilst No 429 would have to wait until March.
D. E. Canning

From May 1970 the Liverpool–Manchester Victoria line as far as Parkside West Junction was used as the routeing for Liverpool–Glasgow trains. On 4 May 1972 No 428 passes Broad Green on the 08.15 Glasgow Central–Liverpool Lime Street, rostered for a single Class 50.
David Rapson

power very difficult, because the duration of full-power running was so short. Part of the problem arose from interruptions caused by signals. The following table gives the percentage of full load during No 409's run.

Section	Time (min)	% under full power
Crewe–Preston	42	34%
Preston–Carlisle	88	31%
Carlisle–Glasgow	126	21%
Glasgow–Carlisle	92	29%
Carlisle–Preston	77	30%
Preston–Crewe	45	53%

Note the low load factor in Scotland. One wonders whether this might not have provided an argument for taking off a locomotive at Carlisle and attaching it to a southbound express, thus reducing the number of units needed for the services with accelerated timings. Between Preston and Carlisle time was lost both northbound and southbound, the schedules being 75 and 76 minutes respectively, though the motive power was not responsible.

A point of concern was that No 409's engine gradually developed less power as the two journeys progressed. This was manifested in a drop-off in maximum engine speed. Accelerating out of Crewe, the peak was 845rpm. Up Shap and

Beattock (with speed falling), top speeds were 785 and 810rpm. In the up direction, climbing the Clyde Valley saw maxima of 850-862rpm, but climbing Shap the peak had fallen to 828 before Penrith and 817 afterwards. At the start of each run No 409 was developing 2,700bhp. Accelerating out of Carlisle at 828rpm the figure was 2,580. Climbing Shap and Beattock, with speed falling, the bhp figures were 2,350 and 2,450.

During its journeys No 413 was found to be delivering a steady 2,600bhp at 870rpm whilst climbing Beattock, but this was the only location where test results were provided. With 850rpm being the normal maximum, it seems unlikely this locomotive was suffering a similar decline in top engine speed to that encountered on No 409.

Both locomotives were said to have run 11,000 hours from new, although the engines installed at the time (IH6934 and IH6940) were not those originally fitted and had been swapped as part of the cylinder-head change programme.

Just why engine top revs declined as the journey progressed was not fully explained by the report, yet this fault amounted to a loss of between 100 and 150bhp. Faults in the control system or governor were postulated. Note the measured 'top of the governor band' effect in No 409's results. With speed falling

Even further south, Nos 50038 and 50022 creep round the Northwich-avoiding line on a Sunday diversion on 21 April 1974. *David Rapson*

whilst climbing Shap and Beattock, power was 200-300bhp below that measured during periods of acceleration.

Fouling of the turbochargers, with implications for combustion air supply to the cylinders, was thought to be the most likely cause of high cylinder temperatures. This fouling was put down to modification of the turbocharger's air-inlet arrangements, which had been effected to reduce engine-room fumes. These fumes were part of a wider problem concerning engine-room air management. A year after the above report into piston problems was drafted, the Service Problems Working Group (SPWG), which embraced representatives from BR HQ, the LMR, British Rail Engineering Ltd (BREL) Crewe and EE, delivered a report on Class 50 ventilation, filtration and contamination. Before the reasons for its production and findings are considered, it should be recalled that this subject had been debated during the design phase: during pre-release works trials at Vulcan No D400 had been found to be right on the limit in terms of engine-room air supply, and Nos D410 and 414

had been modified during construction, to improve air flow and so prevent a build-up of filth inside the locomotive.

The November 1971 report runs to over 60 pages and thus can be dealt with here only in outline. It was commissioned because the poor availability at the time was partly due to the poor performance of the internal air-management arrangements. Although earlier experiments and modifications had brought some improvement, this had been insufficient to give better availability. The main finding was that the inertial filters worked within their design parameters by removing dirt down to five microns in size but that, unfortunately, the particles causing the problem were smaller than four microns. Principal source of these was the engine exhaust, because the exhaust ports were close to the filter intakes. In short, the filters sucked in exhaust because the intakes had been located in the wrong place. Exhaust gases comprised a greasy, sooty mixture that clogged the filters and coated everything inside the locomotive.

Whilst a coating of oily dirt on the interior bodysides and engine was extremely unpleasant as a working environment, it was a recipe for disaster for the main generator and traction motors. The blowers for No 1 and No 6 motors delivered this air mix, and the result, as with the main generator, was a much greater risk of a flashover. With narrower commutator bars than on equivalent Brush electrical machines, the EE products were more prone to brush sparking. Such sparks need not be serious provided the commutator area is clean, but on Class 50 this was not so, and hence flashovers were common.

Worse, oil and coolant leakage from other components dripped into the main generator and caused either earth faults or, in conjunction with brush sparks, significant fires. Such earth faults and fire damage were expensive to repair and involved a visit to Crewe Works for component change that meant a loss of availability. Clogging of the inertial-filter mazes cut engine air supply. This was important for combustion (as noted above), because a reduction meant engine power would decline whilst piston life would be shortened.

The original idea of a sealed engine room had been quickly abandoned, and a grille added to the roof during 1968. The high interior temperatures also caused failure of the radiator-fan resistances due to overheating. Resolution came by pinning open the top two blades on the 'A'-bank radiator shutters to maintain a permanent flow of air. The compressor filters served to spread oil throughout the locomotive, and it was not unknown for oil mist to come out of the AWS horn.

It was recognised that very little could be done to improve the primary or secondary filtration arrangements. Crewe depot removed the inertial filters at the 'E' examination (halfway between works overhauls) but had only limited success with cleaning, using a cold-water pressure washer; Crewe Works used a proprietary chemical and had greater success. Peter Meredith later learned that Eastleigh Works used sodium gluconate for cleaning Class 33 radiators, and this was tried with complete success by Crewe on the inertial filters.

More attention was also given to sealing off the main generator from leaking fluids; this, of course, was partly a design point and partly a maintenance one. Engine-room cleanliness was not helped by the fact the engine itself was a big, 'sweaty' beast. The oil breathers emitted oily fumes, and pipework leaks allowed exhaust gases to escape. Whilst not overtly critical of maintenance standards, comments were made about a greater need to check for oil leaks generally, both before and after attention to the engine – all very depressing and a recipe for problems continuing for years to come.

Proof that the issue of main-generator failure continued to rumble on is provided by the decision to record all flashovers between entry into traffic and January 1973. Clearly these varied as to cause and, as noted in Chapter 3, may have been due to a loose connection on a traction motor. Nevertheless, by December 1969 failures on Nos 408 and 418 were severe enough to warrant a component change in Crewe Works, both locomotives being out of traffic for a month. When the 'V' ring and commutator on its main generator partly disintegrated on 2 February 1970 No 404 was sent to works for a light overhaul – the first time a generator failure had been instrumental in a Class 50 being 'shopped', although over the years this would often prove to be the trigger for such a visit.

During 1972 – the year after the SPWG report on air management – only one main generator failed due to the ingress of coolant or oil, so the report's recommendations did bring some progress. Nevertheless, six machines

The overnight 'Royal Highlander', from Euston to Inverness, was the first scheduled service on which the class appeared. A dishevelled No 439 has just arrived at Perth at 04.30 from Crewe and is waiting to be replaced by a pair of Type 2s for the continuation over the Highland line on 27 June 1971. Pictures of the class here are extremely rare and it was only at this time of year that a photograph could be obtained in daylight. *David N. Clough*

suffered earth faults, four requiring works repair that usually took a month to complete. Despite all the difficulties, everyone acknowledged that the fleet was being worked very hard. Running gear (bogies) would not last between overhauls because of the high miles being run. It therefore became the practice to exchange bogies whilst Crewe depot was carrying out the half-life 'E' exam. This, however, was the only major component change handled on an LMR depot. Eventually, in April 1974, a working party of the SPWG was set up to examine the reasons for the bogies' failure to last 'shop to shop', given that 'Deltic' bogies on the ER did so after a greater mileage. Minor design differences between Class 50 and the nominally similar Class 37 and 55 bogies was a factor, and several changes were implemented to get more life out of those under Class 50. However, it was the WR that would ultimately benefit from these improvements.

Further examination of the Class 50 repair records is illuminating. During this period a system of light and intermediate overhauls comprised the works regime. The planned pattern was light, intermediate, light, general, after 10,000, 20,000, 30,000 and 40,000 engine hours respectively; 10,000 engine hours equated roughly to 7,500 duty hours in the pre-TOPS era. A light overhaul was budgeted to take 12½ days, and an intermediate 34. In fact, the average time on works was actually 41 and 46 days respectively. Nevertheless, this was quite a quick turnaround, when compared with a month for just an unscheduled main-generator change. It was, however, commonplace for a locomotive to have to return to works for rectification, and, being unplanned, this could take up to a month. From the start of classified works repairs in 1969 until 31 March 1973, 4,950 locomotive days were spent on Crewe Works. Of these, 2,662 were spent carrying out classified overhauls and 2,288 unplanned work, including rectification. A total of 174 visits equates to an average of 28

Class 50s gather at Carlisle on 22 February 1974. No 50024 has arrived on the 09.28 from Crewe whilst Nos 50008 and 405 head the 08.00 Euston–Glasgow Central.
David N. Clough

days per locomotive visit. The planned interval between overhauls was, on average, being met.

No 415 was the first to have a light overhaul, entering works on 17 November 1969, and this lasted two months. By October 1970 six of the fleet were in works for light overhauls, with a further example being rectified after such a visit. None of these was shopped following a main-generator failure. EE's 84% availability guarantee had been based on only two receiving works overhauls at any one time, yet here a further five (10%) were out of service for this reason. No 449 was the only other example in works that month, its main generator having shorted and needing changing.

AVAILABILITY GUARANTEE ANALYSED

A clearer picture of why 84% availability was proving hard to achieve thus emerges. Frankly, EE's estimate of only two locomotives at a time in works just does not look realistic. Taking an average time for a light and intermediate of two months, if two class members were in works together it would take 50 months to complete an overhaul cycle. At no time did the class ever run for this interval between shops, and during the period covered by

the availability guarantee the interval was normally half that time.

Other writers have stated that the various engine problems resulted in there being only 48 serviceable power units at one stage, due to the writing-off of two units, but this seems unlikely for several reasons. First, EE had supplied two spare engine-and-generator sets as part of the original contract, making a pool of 52. To end up with only 48 would mean four (not two) had been lost. Looking at the list of engine numbers supplied, only IH6941 disappeared, as noted in Chapter 3. When DP2 was dismantled in 1970, its power unit, IH5567, was overhauled and joined the Class 50 pool. In April 1974 the purchase of two further units – Nos IH7319 and IH7331 – was sanctioned to bolster the reserve; the aim was to keep time on works to a minimum, because an overhauled unit would always be on hand. Engine IH5567, meanwhile, went initially into No 417, during a light overhaul completed on 25 January 1971.

Throughout the early 1970s the number of locomotives on works was generally much higher than envisaged. Although 10 during October 1970 seems to be the peak, to find eight or nine in Crewe from 1971 to 1973 was common. Clearly this did not help availability. Once BREL was formed to

With the M6 motorway in the background, No 417 storms through Newton-le-Willows with the 09.28 all-stations Crewe–Carlisle on 21 October 1972. This locomotive was the only one fitted with weight-transfer-compensation equipment. *David N. Clough*

take over all BR's works facilities, Crewe was no longer under the control of the LMR. Such autonomy meant it could devise its own work programmes, and dealing with unscheduled appearances of Class 50s was a low priority. The LMR was unhappy with the standard of service, its engineers believing that during this period the Works was more interested in overhauling bus engines (under a new contract) than doing railway work. Eventually the priority arrangement already in place at Doncaster for dealing with 'Deltic' repairs was adopted at Crewe Works for Class 50.

Other problems also affected performance, but space here precludes further detailed consideration. Several are worth mentioning in brief, however. Tyre fracturing was blamed on the dynamic-brake equipment, but this system was proved under trials to be very effective. Removal of the bottom piston-scraper ring caused oil to pass into the combustion chamber and be discharged through the exhaust, and on 28 December 1970 an indignant passenger did not take too kindly when No 404 spat oil over his suit! Oil also ran down the bodyside exterior, helping dirt stick and making the locomotives filthy. Elsewhere on the engine, turbochargers began to fail, for several reasons. None of these helped availability; for the last nine full months of

fleet allocation to the WCML (to the end of April 1974) availability was a pitiful 65.5%, though reliability was up to 14,500mpc.

As stated earlier, under the availability guarantee EE was obliged to pay BR £50 per locomotive short of the 84% target each day. Study of the availability figures quoted above suggests EE was having an expensive time of it. A BR report of 1973 estimated that between 1 January 1969 and 31 March 1973 an average of 10 locomotives above the contracted eight had been unavailable. Based on £50 per locomotive per day, BR had a maximum possible claim of £775,000. To that date, BR had claimed just £60,650, with responsibility for non-availability assigned 92% to BR and 8% to EE.

Analysis of a four-week period from 13 August 1972 shows why the BR claim was so low. The average number of units out of service each day was 18, yet the claim against EE was only £300. There had been 24 instances where more than the contracted seven locomotives were stopped for scheduled depot and works exams. Over the 28 days there were 76 instances of stoppages being due to 'awaiting staff' – in other words, locomotives not being worked on and thus BR's responsibility. There were 65 entries of 'awaiting materials', also BR's fault. EE was no longer carrying stocks of certain components and so manufactured to order. Lead times had shot up from three months in 1971 to 16 months in 1973, due partly to lengthy industrial disputes at both Vulcan and Trafford Park.

In truth, BR eventually acknowledged that the contract wording was imprecise and that there was ambiguity surrounding the basis for the calculation, as well as who was responsible for non-availability. A report from the LMR's CMEE to his BRB opposite number highlights this with these figures:

Period	LMR calculation	EE calculation
31/1/70-2/1/71	£27,700	£16,800
30/1/71-2/1/72	£20,320	£6,500

There had been debate as to whether the 84% guarantee changed when more than five locomotives were stopped for scheduled depot maintenance or two for works overhaul. Maintenance schedules had been drawn up by EE but with influence from the LMR, based on experience with other EE diesels. BR had finally accepted that if more programmed (as opposed to unplanned due to failure) maintenance caused more than these numbers of the class to be sidelined, then this was not EE's fault. For 1972 this was estimated to have saved EE £13,000 (equal to 260 locomotive days). That it just was not practical to overhaul only two machines at a time has been explained above. Clearly it had also been found that depot examinations could not be done at the correct interval if only five were stopped for this purpose.

OTHER OPERATIONS

Whilst the double-headed duties naturally captured the limelight, the class continued to be busy on other services, though not with the same degree of diversity as prior to May 1970. Of interest were No 423 on the 12.50 Dundee–Glasgow Queen Street on 9 June 1971 and No 424 on the up 'Thames–Clyde Express' (piloting a Class 46 through to Leeds) on 2 July. On 28 October 1973 the class made its debut at Nuneaton, dragging diverted Trent Valley services from Stafford via Wolverhampton and the

Class 50s spent a lot of time other than on passenger duties, newspaper, mail and parcels services being far more common in the early 1970s than they are today. In the autumn of 1971 an unidentified example brings the lengthy 10.23 Heysham–Manchester Victoria vans past Bolton West 'box, as a 'white stripe' BRCW Class 104 DMU departs for Blackpool North. *David N. Clough*

route from Saltley, Nos 402, 433 and 443 being so employed. Similar Sunday engineering activity frequently saw a class member towing a dead electric and its train out of Manchester Piccadilly and Liverpool Lime Street, sometimes over exotic routes. Equally, closure of the WCML meant that paired '50' services penetrated unlikely haunts in East Manchester, such as Ashton Moss, whilst picking their way between Crewe and Preston.

Reports show a regular presence east of Perth on trains through Dundee and Dunfermline. These were in addition to Perth's use of the locomotive off the overnight Euston–Inverness (and stabled there during the day) for passenger turns to Edinburgh; when, from early 1974, the '50' began to work through to Inverness, Perth lost this facility.

RUNNING PRE-ELECTRIFICATION

From 23 July 1973 electrification work had advanced to the point that traction-changing became possible at Preston. This did not happen with all trains, because the need to get Class 50s back to Crewe for maintenance remained. From this date accelerated-timings services were allowed 44min when diesel-hauled or 36min with an electric. That the latter was virtually impossible with the booked load and a Class 86 is another story.

Undoubtedly the fastest running north of Crewe became possible in the week or so before the new 'Electric Scot' timetable commenced in May 1974. This was because speed limits were raised and 100mph became the norm, while intermediate restrictions were less severe. Of course, liberal amounts of recovery time remained in the schedules to compensate for electrification work, and some drivers chose to moderate their running to avoid getting ahead of time. Nevertheless, with 80mph now permitted over Shap, it was possible to see how fast a pair could climb the bank without being restricted. In addition, single locomotives on accelerated workings could be stretched to the limit. North of Preston, a personal run behind No 50021 with 12 coaches (430 tons gross) was matched very closely by one timed by Michael Oakley with No 50022.

Stand clear from the platform edge or prepare to be spattered with oil from No 50046! The tell-tale stain down the bodyside indicates oil is passing the cylinders and being vented through the exhaust. Nos 50044 and 50046 back onto the 14.05 Euston–Glasgow Central at Preston on 6 April 1974; extension of electrification to Preston in July 1973 saw many trains change traction there in consequence. *David N. Clough*

On the 14.05 ex Euston on 4 May 1974 No 50021 passed Lancaster inside the 18min booked. With an 89mph maximum at Carnforth, speed was still 71 at Oxenholme and 55.5 over Grayrigg. From 84mph through Tebay, speed had been brought down to 49 by Shap, and the time to the summit was 50min 30sec. By comparison, the run with No 409 described earlier took 52min 40sec. Although No 50021 was one minute late here, the driver took things easily down to Carlisle because of the 14min recovery time in the schedule. Arrival was in 75min 39sec (72min net), compared to 86min booked, No 50021 having thus dropped just 3min 30sec on a timing based on a pair.

On the up road, also on 4 May, No 50035 turned in one of its customary outstanding performances from Glasgow to Preston on the 13.55 departure. Again, the load was 12 for around 425 tons gross. The only impedance to Carlisle was a signal check at Larkfield Junction, and between Beattock and Gretna Junction average speed was 90mph, with a maximum of 101. Arrival at the Border City was thus six minutes to the good, in under 85min. Storming up Shap, 74mph was attained before Penrith. Then came a long-standing track-slowing near Eden Valley Junction. The descent of Shap produced 100mph before Tebay and 98 near Burton, followed by a further pws at Bolton le Sands. A flat-out effort on the final leg to Preston was

eschewed in order to avoid too early an arrival, but the running time was still just 80min 1sec – 9min early. Allowing for the delays, the net time from Carlisle was 76min, as opposed to 71min net for two locomotives. No wonder the LMR judged this machine capable of handling the accelerated timings single-handed!

Whilst contemporary recordings suggest most of the class (such as Nos 50021/2/35 singled out above) were delivering normal power, the odd one could do even better, though a few were certainly rogues. On 18 April 1974 No 50023 was, unusually, turned out for railtour duty on the Wirral Railway Circle's 'Alstonian' charter. Whilst the slog up from Settle Junction to Blea Moor saw just 1,970rhp (2,590bhp), accelerating out of Carlisle coaxed a spectacular 2,230rhp (2,900bhp). However, it should be remembered the control system delivered peak performance only during acceleration and not during deceleration under full power. By contrast, on 3 May 1974 (and again corroborated by a similar run timed by Michael Oakley) No 50012 showed a dreadful standard. By way of example, on the climb southbound to Shap, only 1,660rhp (2,170bhp) was produced, and even adding 100hp for possible train heat makes little difference. Illustrating how this low power translates into slower running, the following table compares No 50012 with No 50035, both with the same loads.

	50012	50035
Motherwell–Carluke	9min 12sec	8min 44sec
Carlisle–Penrith	21min 13sec	18min 49sec
Lancaster–Barton	13min	12min

Mr Davies says that reports of low power with no obvious cause could still result in use of the load bank. With availability under 70%, downtime for an operational locomotive to carry out a load bank test must have been a fine judgement, and there may have been occasions when drivers had to make the best of it. The exhaust system was very prone to air leakage at its many joints, and this would cause air pressure to the turbochargers to drop; this would be detected by the engine governor, and the latter's boost-bias protection system would then reduce the engine output. With exhaust leaks quite common, this could explain instances of low power.

Some locomotives clearly suffered low power on a regular basis, as this amusing story demonstrates. To repeated entries by a driver in a locomotive repair book relating to loss of power or low power, depot staff had responded with just as many entries of 'Tested – NFF' (no fault found). The driver, after experiencing yet another occurrence on the offending locomotive, wrote: 'See Hebrews Chapter 13, Verse 8.' On checking the depot Bible (!) the staff found: 'Jesus Christ, the same yesterday, and today, and for ever'!

With No 50012, matters were made worse because its speedometer was clearly over-recording in habitual Class 50 tradition. EE speedos were never as accurate as the Hawker Siddeley equivalents fitted to Class 47, and this so often meant speed never hit the 100mph mark, because the driver was misled as to the true speed. This issue would recur on the WR, where sustained top-speed running was practical but not as common as it should have been.

DOWNGRADING

In early 1974 BR bought the entire fleet. Just when this happened, why it happened and whether BR or EE initiated the transaction are not known. However, there was no provision in the

In the months before the introduction of the full 'Electric Scot' timetable in May 1974 the use of a single machine (instead of a pair) became more common. On 30 March 1974 No 50009 passes Carnforth on time with the 13.55 Glasgow–Euston. *David N. Clough*

Left: From May 1974 the balance of operations for the surviving LMR allocation swung towards freight. One of the remaining regular Class 1 jobs was a diagram between Liverpool Lime Street and Preston, where an electric took over for the continuation to Glasgow Central. On 20 March 1975 No 50010 would have had little difficulty on the sharp climb through Rainhill with the short 12.41 Lime Street–Edinburgh Waverley. *David Rapson*

Below: The corresponding workings from Manchester Victoria to Preston, where trains often combined with a Liverpool portion, were also regularly '50'-powered. In April 1975 a Sunday diversion brought No 50040 into Wigan Wallgate on such a service. *David Cross*

Diesel required to drag an
electric and its train on a
Sunday diversion? Step forward
Class 50! On 27 July 1975
No 50036 'tops' No 86007 with
a Liverpool Lime Street–Euston
train routed via Chester and
recorded at Calveley.
David Rapson

Class 50 contract for such a sale, because
BR had merely an option to extend its
lease at the end of the primary lease
period.

From 6 May 1974 the LMR was left with
just 12 examples – Nos 50008/10/2/21/2/9/
31/4-6/41/5. There appears to have been
an error, though, because a fortnight later
Nos 50006/17/40 arrived back at Crewe,
making the total 15. No precise
information on their rostering is to hand,
but clearly it was varied and widespread.
There seemed to be some interchange-
ability with ETH Class 47s on passenger
duties, while the variety of freight turns
covered was the widest ever seen. Space
does not allow the full panoply of these to
be explored, but the regular – and some
very irregular – workings will serve to
illustrate.

On the passenger side, the diagram for
an ETH Type 4 on the Liverpool–Preston
leg of through trains to Glasgow and
Edinburgh was generally assigned to a
Class 50. It is likely that the equivalent
section from Manchester Victoria to
Preston would have featured the type, as
would that forward from Preston to
Blackpool North for through workings
from Euston. The surviving Glasgow–
Euston and return service routed via the
Glasgow & South Western also seemed to

produce a Class 50 as far as Carlisle. The
class is known to have taken over the
'Clansman' (Euston–Inverness) northbound
from the traction-change point of Mossend
Yard. In 1975 Class 40s were finally
displaced from the Londons on the North
Wales Coast; this meant that Class 50s
finally reached Holyhead on a regular
basis, aside from making visits on the
09.20 service as pilot to the train engine,
when undertaking a trial run from either
Crewe Depot or Works.

Some remarkable feats of running were
reported during this period. A mystery
excursion from Blackpool to Arrochar was
powered by No 50036 as far as Mossend
Yard; with 11 coaches, the diesel is
claimed to have covered the Preston–
Carlisle leg in 71min 30sec, which effort
should be judged against those of
paired '50s' described earlier. Shortage of
electric power on 17 October 1974 saw
No 50040 – another redoubtable
performer – deputise on the 1M27
Glasgow–Liverpool/Manchester, reported
passing Gretna Junction only 2min down
on electric timings.

Looking at freight activity, the 7M49
Cardiff–Carlisle and balancing 7V57
Carlisle–Severn Tunnel Junction remained
Class 50-powered, as they had been since
1968. Shortage of electric traction also

Left: **Company 'liner' trains were also diagrammed for Class 50 until electric traction took over, and in the first couple of months after electrification a shortage of Class 87s required Class 50s to deputise on these services. No 50031 storms past Springs Branch with a late-running 22.20 Linwood–Gosford Green Chrysler service on 20 August 1974.**
David N. Clough collection

Below: **A considerable number of partially-fitted freights had to be routed via the Settle line after all catch points over Shap were removed. Preferred traction was, of course, Class 50. No 50021 drifts down past Settle Junction on 14 September 1974 with a service from Carlisle to the WR.**
David N. Clough collection

impacted on long-haul freights too, notably the Chrysler company services between Gosford Green and Linwood. It seems a Class 50 was the preferred diesel deputy, if one was to hand.

During their final years on the LMR, as well as frequenting their established stamping-grounds, the Class 50s continued to break new territory. Allan Baker reports that use on merry-go-round (MGR) work before May 1974 was generally confined to trial runs for locomotives off maintenance at Crewe, when they could not be trusted on a passenger duty. After that date, however, they regularly visited Fiddler's Ferry, Rugeley and Ironbridge power stations, on coal trains originating from Silverdale, Trentham, Bickershaw, Bold and Cronton collieries. With a typical 33-wagon consist, the trailing load would have been upwards of 1,500 tons – the heaviest tackled single-handed by the type.

During the summer of 1975 the usual Class 25 on the Winsford rock-salt service to Tweedmouth often gave way to a Class 50, and these trains, in common with occasional others, brought the class to Tyne Yard. The type also appeared on services to Shotton Steelworks via Middlewich and Mickle Trafford and on Cumbrian Coast freights. In Scotland, Falkland Yard, Ayr, received regular visits, whilst they were familiar sights across the Lowland belt, even reaching Edinburgh. Mundane in the extreme was the use on

5 April 1976 of 100mph, ETH-equipped No 50031 on an engineer's demolition train along the surviving spur of the former Midland Railway route from Lancaster Green Ayre towards Wennington. During their final few years on the LMR it really was a case of no job too big or small. The curtain really came down in May 1976, when the last three examples migrated to Plymouth Laira.

Crewe Works continued to be responsible for works repairs until December 1976, and the LMR was not shy in borrowing a newly overhauled locomotive. Several instances are on record of WR-allocated engines revisiting old haunts in the North West. When BR wanted to carry out high-speed trials north of Crewe in connection with the Advanced Passenger Train, the WR loaned Nos 50036 and 50045 for the purpose. Reputedly, speeds up to 110mph were attained between Lancaster and Southwaite, near Carlisle, and it is possible this was the occasion when an unauthorised maximum of 115mph was reached. According to the report, a pair of '50s', with test coach behind, achieved said speed before stopping at Preston; however, on the descent from Coppull the leading locomotive's speedometer failed, and unfortunately the telephone link between test car and driving cab was not working, so the staff in the former could not advise the driver just how fast he was travelling.

Left: **Train 7V57 – the 08.30 Registered Wagon Service from Carlisle to Severn Tunnel Junction – was regularly loaded to 50 short-wheelbase vans and was a very reliable and punctual runner. No 50031 passes Houghton Summit on 27 August 1974.** *David Rapson*

Below: **After May 1974 the LMR made use of Class 50's slow-speed-control facility when a Class 47 was unavailable for merry-go-round work. On 15 August 1974 No 50035 coasts towards Newton-le-Willows with the 10.13 from Bickershaw Colliery to Fiddler's Ferry power station.** *David N. Clough*

Right: **Not all freight turns were associated with the WCML. More usually Class 40-powered, the 8E34 Garston–Wombwell coal empties brought No 50010 onto the now closed Liverpool–Manchester freight route at Thelwall on 9 October 1974. The '50' would have given way to a pair of Class 76 electrics at Godley.** *David Rapson*

Below: **Between 1974 and 1976 no job was too big or too small for an LMR Class 50. Falling into the latter category was this task for No 50034, seen coming off the WCML at Salop Goods Junction on the Crewe Independent lines with two Class 27s and a green Class 47 – all bound for works – in tow.** *David N. Clough*

5

Transfer to the WR

EARLY DUTIES

The National Traction Plan of the late 1960s had sealed the fate of the WR's diesel-hydraulic classes, and it was only a matter of time before all were withdrawn. The last to be replaced were the Class 52 'Westerns', of 2,700bhp nominal rating, though probably 2,760bhp in actuality. Nos 1019 and 1032 were the first to succumb, on 7 May 1973, and BR decided that Class 50 should act as replacement power once West Coast electrification was complete. The BRB's intention was to provide the WR with traction capable of 100mph running for the London–Bristol/ West of England routes, and this was to be in the form of Class 50s, possibly working in pairs.

Reallocation of the class began on 11 October 1972, when No 400 was sent to Bristol Bath Road for driver training. On the 19th it hauled a seven-coach train from Bristol to Taunton and back, to train traction inspectors. On 25 November No 400 made the class debut at Old Oak Common, whilst on the 30th it was noted heading west through Teignmouth. Paddington was reached for the first time on 1 December, again on a special. (It was station staff at Paddington who dubbed the class 'Hoovers', because of the sound made by air passing over the inertial-filter fins; this nickname stuck for many years, unlike 'bleeps', used by LMR staff.) The first use on a scheduled train out of the terminus occurred on 15 January 1973 on the 17.12 to Weston-super-Mare.

No 401 joined No 400 in July, and No 402 followed in November, both being allocated to Bath Road. No 400 then moved to Plymouth Laira, whilst No 401 was moved to Old Oak Common in December, thus spreading the opportunities for staff training. It seems the first WR diagram was assigned in August, as illustrated in the box (right).

No 427 made the class debut at Penzance on 19 March 1974, within days of arriving on the Region. As late as 4 April no decision had been reached as to how many or which of the class would be going west. One suggestion was that numerical order would decide the transfers, but this was ruled out because it was felt better that the LMR should monitor existing experiments in progress on certain machines. Peter Meredith has since admitted privately that he kept the 'best' after May, ensuring that problem locomotives disappeared from the LMR's books.

Over the weekend of 4/5 May locomotives reallocated made their way in twos and threes via the North & West route through Hereford. From the start of the Summer 1974 timetable on the 6th, Class 50s monopolised the London–Bristol duties (upon which they were judged five minutes faster than Class 47 – a claim that will be explored further in Chapter 7), with some running to the West Country. A cross-country turn, involving the 07.40 Penzance–Liverpool as far as Birmingham and the 15.15 return, was also rostered. Initially Bath Road had 20 examples, Laira 10 and Old Oak Common five.

WR IN TROUBLE

Perhaps understandably, the class was a bit of a handful for drivers and maintenance staff with no previous experience of electronic control systems. Early LMR experiences were therefore repeated, with many failures reported during the first few months of squadron service. Of course, the hydraulic fanatics, regarding the '50s' as responsible for the demise of their beloved (but expensive) 'Westerns', delighted in reporting every

M-F	08.05 and 15.15 Bristol–Paddington and 11.45 and 18.45 returns
SO	08.07 Weston-super-Mare–Paddington and 14.16 return
SuO	17.45 Bristol–Paddington and 22.45 return

problem. The same people tried to make out that the (relatively) low maximum starting tractive effort for the class meant climbing the South Devon banks would be an impossibility. This, of course, overlooked the fact that 850-ton trains had been hauled daily over the steepest climbs on the WCML. Such is irrational partisanship.

Engineers on the LMR confirm that an offer was made to the WR to send its personnel to Crewe depot prior to May 1974. The objective (as the LMR saw it) was to gain first-hand experience of living with the '50s'. Independent to the last, the WR spurned this offer. To be fair, the WR was having a pretty rough time. Taking the period from May 1975 to January 1976 (when data for the LMR ceased to be compiled) the availability and reliability figures for each Region's fleet were:

	LMR	WR
Availability (%)	76.9	58.4
Reliability (mpc)	26,252	9,250

These show a remarkable transformation for the LMR, when compared to the details

for the nine months to April 1974 (set out in Chapter 4). Who said hard work never killed anyone? The easier regime post May 1974 definitely brought better performance. Based on a sample of four locomotives, the LMR fleet was now running 76,000 miles per annum – considerably below the 105,000 of 1971.

The poor WR was clearly going through the mill with its new acquisitions, but by the SPWG meeting on 5 December 1974 the Region was confident that staff familiarisation was no longer a factor. In truth, this may have been rather optimistic, because silly failures were still occurring a decade later, and it had taken the LMR much longer than eight months to get everyone conversant with the new motive power. Minutes of the SPWG for 22 May 1975 point the finger for poor availability at Crewe Works, where eight (22%) of the WR's stud were undergoing attention (see the box on the far right).

Only two of these were receiving a classified overhaul, while two were having to be rectified after a classified overhaul, and four were there for unplanned repairs. Adding to its woes,

The 'Golden Hind' business service to Plymouth and Penzance from the capital was a '50' turn. The down service is captured pounding uphill near Thatcham. *D. E. Canning*

the WR also cited a shortage of spares as affecting availability.

In contrast, the only example of the LMR's remaining 14-strong stud to spend any time on works during the first half of 1975 was No 50031, for bodywork repair. In defence of Crewe Works, however, it must be said that the arrival of four unplanned visitors would have done nothing for workload scheduling. Nevertheless, No 50030 was stopped at Crewe from 2 February 1976 until 28 January 1977 just for repair to a main generator – rather excessive!

As was the case before on the LMR, there were several technical issues at the centre of the poor performance. Main generators continued to give trouble, and component shortages due to repair lead times caused some locomotives to be stopped on works awaiting an overhauled replacement. There was nothing new in the cause of these failures, water and oil ingress being a major factor. For the first time, however, it was suggested Crewe Works could not carry out the repairs properly where re-insulation was needed.

Power-earth faults were becoming an increasingly common cause of failure.

These could occur in any of a number of circuits, and the WR sought to eliminate as many redundant (as it saw them) systems as possible. Jumper-connecting ports were sealed up, the dynamic-brake gear was isolated and the tractive-effort control taken out of use; in so doing, it reduced fitter time in tracing earth faults.

Turbocharger surging (or buffeting) remained a problem. Part of the cause was thought at first to be insufficient air supply, and this was put down to inadequate air flow when the inertial filters were dirty. Tests showed a 100bhp difference in engine output after the filters were just pressure washed. Inadequate air-flow also meant over-fuelling of the engine, because

50015 (light, 24 April to 26 May)
50016 (unclassified repair, power unit and body, 21 April to 30 May)
50018 (unclassified repair, power unit 21 May to 14 June)
50021 (unclassified repair, power unit 12 May to 19 June)
50025 (rectification after intermediate, second time, power unit, 5 May to 24 June)
50032 (unclassified repair, 18 February to 15 May)
50038 (intermediate overhaul, 18 February to 10 May)
50047 (rectification after intermediate overhaul, 15 April to 22 May)

Above: **Paignton had a frequent Summer Saturdays link from London. On 2 July 1975 No 50038 provides the power for the 16.30 down, seen passing one of Exeter St Davids' magnificent signal gantries.** *Dave Mitchell*

Right: **Limited daily use on cross-country services from the West Country to Birmingham started in 1974. No 50019 coasts past Lawrence Hill, outside Bristol Temple Meads, with the 1V92 10.06 Edinburgh–Plymouth on 30 May 1974. This train later became the usual means of returning an overhauled locomotive from Doncaster to the WR, but in 1974 the appearance of a Class 50 was highly unusual.** *David Rapson*

When BR abandoned use of the headcode boxes, Class 50s carried '0000' for a time before marker lights were fitted. No 50039 calls at Newbury in charge of the 16.53 Paddington–Plymouth on 21 January 1976. *D. E. Canning*

there was not enough air for combustion of all the fuel oil supplied. In addition the turbochargers were becoming fouled with oil, and this impaired their performance. Surging, due to over-fuelling, caused failures of the impeller blades, and different grades of oil were trialled to address the issue.

By December 1975 it was thought that the surging was due to the engine's developing too much power. This had been suspected back in 1968 when locomotives that were reported to be surging were found to be producing high engine power on Crewe depot's load bank. No 50038 was singled out in the minutes of the SPWG meeting of 11 March 1976 as being especially prone to surging between the second and third stages of field weakening; it had been released from an intermediate on 10 May 1975 and was load-bank-tested at Cardiff Canton in early 1976. A further view on surging was put forward at the March 1977 SPWG meeting; this time blame was attributed to turbocharger charge air and engine speed being too high.

It seems that during the late 1970s (and possibly into the 1980s) Laira decided unilaterally to derate Class 50 engines in an attempt to reduce turbocharger failures. Bath Road felt that it was evident that the fuel-rack settings were being tampered with to reduce power. Examples of its own allocation that had visited Laira were found to have been so adjusted, but the Bristol depot returned its machines to the correct setting, though it did leave Laira's allocation at the derated setting. This derating has always been officially denied, though measured road performance supports the case for tampering having taken place.

The main issue, however, concerned traction-motor failures, which peaked during 1975, when an average of 13 motors per month had to be changed. The source of the problem was a design change made by EE to simplify production and possibly improve commutation; this saw the previous solid conductors on the armatures changed for a split type which had a tendency to 'lift' during prolonged high-speed running and resulted in chafing of the windings, which then led to flashovers. To be fair to the WR, its operating regime represented the first time Class 50 had run at around 100mph for sustained periods; this had never been possible on the LMR. The solution, after trials of various different types of motor brush, was to exchange armatures between Class 50 and Class 37. Motors were dealt with in batches of six (enough for a complete locomotive), and the work was shared between Crewe and Doncaster, which had works responsibility for the two classes. No 50037, at Crewe for an intermediate overhaul from 24 July 1974, was the first to receive solid conductor armatures.

Main-generator failures continued to plague availability for a further five years, until the refurbishment programme (dealt with in Chapter 6) had been completed. Meanwhile, from the end of 1976, Doncaster took over the mantle of responsibility for works repairs and overhauls. No 50036 was the last to receive a classified overhaul at Crewe, departing on 31 December. It was not the last Class 50 on the Works, however; No 50030's presence has

already been noted, but the honour of being the last of the class to be repaired there went to No 50038, which came on works on 8 December 1976 for engine and main-generator repairs and left on 17 February 1977.

DONCASTER WORKS

As part of work-scheduling within the BREL workshops, the synergy between Class 50 and Classes 37 and 55 brought about a change of works responsibility from Crewe to Doncaster. Following proper consideration, Doncaster was going to carry out classified overhauls in a timescale of between six and eight weeks, and only two examples would therefore need to be stopped at a time. Alas for such optimism, because such a turnaround was never remotely achieved over the next decade and, looking on as an outsider, one wonders who accepted this as feasible, and why, when the past six years' experience clearly showed it was not.

No 50009 had the honour of being the first to go to 'The Plant'; having departed

Showing the blank screen that began to appear in the headcode box c1977, No 50040 battles through snow at Witham on the Berks & Hants line.
D. E. Canning

Laira on 23 December 1976, it spent Christmas at Old Oak Common and reportedly arrived at Doncaster (via Finsbury Park) on the 29th. Of course, the works had no Class 50 experience, and it was not surprising that a light overhaul took until 10 June 1977 to complete. No 50048 followed soon after for unclassified attention but was instead given a light overhaul which was not completed until 10 February 1978 – 13 months!

On 10 March No 50041 was noted at Temple Mills Yard, East London, *en route* for main-generator repairs, and this was the usual routeing followed by 'dead' locomotives. After its release on 18 May it was used by the ER for crew-training at Doncaster depot: on 27 July it made the class debut at Newcastle on driver training, whilst next day it traversed the Doncaster–Hull line; Peterborough received a visit on 10 August, just days before a readmission to the Works for further power-unit attention. Emerging on 5 October, No 50041 was noted at Newark the same day.

On 10 June No 50009 was seen in the company of No 31268 on the day of its release on the Newcastle–Poole train. Three days later, however, it passed Ferrybridge *en route* to York with an ECS. The ER clearly had confidence in the type, because on the 16th No 50009 took over from a failed Class 47 on the 08.30 from Leeds (08.35 from Hull) to King's Cross and 14.10 return. There was another instance of the ER borrowing a '50' on 14 September, when No 50042 piloted 'Deltic' No 55017 (no doubt in trouble) on the 06.50 Hull–King's Cross. Down the years, some locomotives worked home via the East Coast route, but by far the most common method was to haul the 09.50 Edinburgh–Plymouth forward from the booked traction change at York.

Main generators continued to fail, classified repair cycles continued to come round and Doncaster was still giving priority to scheduled (and often unscheduled) visits by Class 55 'Deltics'. During November Doncaster had accumulated 12 (24% of the fleet) inside its walls; six were receiving light overhauls, one an intermediate and five were in need of replacement main generators. It wasn't as though the stays were short: No 50020 arrived on 20

September for unclassified attention and left on 8 June 1978.

No wonder WR availability was appalling. The SPWG minutes of 23 September 1978 reported that poor performance was due to main generators (awaiting rehabilitation), to fuel-oil and cooling systems and to power units (respectively 10%, 5%, 15% and 5% of casualties); electrical faults were also common, and the locomotives were not being given priority at Doncaster.

Now that the class was BR property, the 'On Hire' plates were removed, many being dumped on the scrap skip at Laira. No 50011 seems to have carried these plates the longest, because these were still in place during the summer of 1979. Also around this time BR dispensed with the use of headcode boxes, and several of the class appeared with an abridged version of their number instead.

OPERATIONS

Throughout the period 1974-80 there were strong rumours of the intended use of Class 50 on the Midland main line, to replace Class 45s that were failing far too often, but eventually HSTs were found for this purpose.

The first double-heading on the WR is reported to have been on 18 May 1974 and

A further slight change in livery came with naming. To make way for the nameplates, the BR emblem was moved from the bodyside to under the secondman's cab window. No 50009 *Conqueror* shows the change as it takes empty stock from Paddington to Old Oak Common on 11 July 1981.
David N. Clough

involved Nos 50025 and 50039 on the 12.15 Paddington–Bristol. In part to evaluate potential time-saving and in part to provide for possible on-line failures, during February and March 1975 the up and down workings of the prestigious 'Golden Hind' service between Paddington and Penzance as far as Plymouth were each assigned two locomotives. A dedicated pool was used to ensure that the multiple-unit jumpers were operable, and class members known to have been used were Nos 50014/26-8/50. The WR had flirted with diesel double-heading previously on passenger trains, trying out pairs of Class 37s and then pairs of Class 42s. Although the extra horsepower did provide some time savings, its use never lasted long enough, and the experiment with Class 50 was no exception.

As a prelude to wider utilisation, No 50050 spent a week at Saltley depot during February 1975. The table below shows a typical six-day roster at this time.

Despite its poor availability, the type was used on freight turns, and these included occasional forays onto the SR on inter-Regional freights in the London area. No 50026 was the first sighting, at Norwood Yard on 19 December 1975. During 1976 haulage of the Acton–St Erth milk tanks and Truro–Exeter Riverside freights was common. A most unusual report claimed

No 50049 passed through Andover on a freight on 1 September.

With new HSTs about to arrive on the WR, plans were put in hand to re-deploy Class 50s that would then be displaced from the Bristol services. During January 1976 Nos 50025 and 50047 were at Worcester for staff-training purposes, so that from the Summer timetable the Type 4s could displace Class 31s on certain Paddington–Worcester turns. (Two months later Nos 50015 and 50025 were at Gloucester for the same reason.) Whilst in the Worcester area, the locomotive from the Paddington train would take a turn on Lickey banking duties between 20.00 and 03.00. Meanwhile the 06.45 Paddington–Birmingham was frequently in the hands of a Class 50, and the Summer timetable also brought the first regular visits to South Wales, courtesy of the 13.15 Paddington–Cardiff and 17.25 return on weekdays.

On 2 June 1976 there was a major incident when No 50019 was derailed at Reading due to a fractured tyre. The report noted that the dynamic brake was inoperative, as was the case on several other class members. It had averaged 95,900 miles per annum since the last works overhaul in November 1973 and had run 791,250 miles from new (average 97,900 per year).

Increasing numbers of HSTs brought a reallocation of the Class 50 fleet; as 1976 came to a close Bath Road had Nos 50037-44/6-9, and Laira the rest. An interim HST timetable had commenced in October 1976, and it was really the arrival of this form of traction (not Class 50, as 'hydraulic' fans like to claim) that saw off the last of the 'Westerns'.

During January 1977 route-learning took place between Leamington Spa, Coventry and Birmingham New Street. This was in conjunction with the opening of Birmingham International and diversion via the Leamington Spa–Coventry freight line of most Paddington–Birmingham services. Curiously, Class 50s were used on the route-learning specials, No 50037 being the first to be observed.

Although squadron HST deployment had been intended from the Summer 1977 timetable, technical problems with the sets meant this did not come about until early 1978. Now that the track-upgrade work for 125mph running was complete, some

Sample Class 50 working, No 50016, 15-20 January 1975

Date	Time	Train
15	03.00	Plymouth–Penzance
	08.35	Penzance–Plymouth
	13.00	Plymouth–Paddington
	18.12	Paddington–Taunton
		Taunton–Bristol Malago Vale (ECS)
16	05.00	Bristol Malago Vale–Taunton (ECS)
	06.43	Taunton–Paddington
	12.15	Paddington–Bristol
	15.15	Bristol–Paddington
	18.30	Paddington–Plymouth
17	05.10	Plymouth–Paddington
	12.15	Paddington–Bristol
	16.15	Bristol–Paddington
	18.27	Paddington–Truro
18		'A' examination at Laira
	10.00	Plymouth–Birmingham
	15.15	Birmingham–Plymouth
19	14.30	Plymouth–Paddington
20	18.30	Paddington–Plymouth

enterprising timings were set for the surviving Class 50-hauled trains on the Bristol road. The 17.20 Paddington–Taunton had a 79mph average to its first stop at Chippenham, while Paddington–Cheltenham trains that made a first call at Swindon were allowed 66min, requiring an average of 70mph. These timings included some recovery time, of course.

Completion of driver-training at Hereford brought this route within Class 50's sphere of operation, while the cascade of air-conditioned coaches onto the principal West Country diagrams strengthened the type's grip on West of England services. The 'Cornish Riviera Express' now took 10min less to Plymouth, now reached in 3hr 40min going down and 3hr 33min up. So the demise of the Class 52 'Westerns' saw the WR's most prestigious working speeded up, not (as sometimes suggested) slowed down!

And how did the rivals square up over the South Devon banks? Generally, of course, speed was falling against the grade. As noted on Shap and Beattock, this was not where a '50' would develop its peak power. In his articles in the *Railway Magazine*, O. S. Nock commented that the fastest runs known to him, based on his own and contributors' timings, gave the advantage to the diesel-electric. Taking the

analysis forward nearly 30 years and into the world of preservation, in 2002 both types ran unaided over the banks with decent loads. Class 52 No 1015 took 12 cars over Dainton at 27mph – very creditable. This does not, however, compare with the achievement of No 50031, which, with an extra coach, cleared the summit at 36. Honours, again, to the '50'. Aside, possibly, from starting heavy stone trains, the much beloved 'Westerns' could not match Class 50s when both types were set up properly.

In fact, the WR's routes generally suited the Class 50 performance characteristics better than did those of the LMR. Leaving aside the West Country, gradients were modest, and trains could be accelerated away from stops and the locomotive left on full power – and with the engine governor at the top of the band; the relatively high speed (87mph) at which main-generator unloading took place allowed much better times and speeds than could be managed by Class 47. Between Paddington and Reading a '50' was the equivalent of a coach better than a '47', or 45sec in overall time. The gain was really between Hanwell and Sonning, where, on identical loads, the former was between 3 and 5mph faster in the 90-100mph bracket.

The quaint buildings at Torquay present almost a model-railway feel, but No 50012 *Benbow*, seen with the 10.30 Paddington–Paignton on 7 April 1980, is certainly full-sized.
David N. Clough

Above: **Following the introduction of increasing numbers of HSTs, Class 50 displaced Type 3 power on the Paddington–Hereford line. The 18.30 up service is seen crossing Ledbury Viaduct on 17 July 1981.** *David N. Clough collection*

Right: **Initially, Motorail services ran as a combined train, comprising passenger stock and flat-bed vehicles on which the cars were carried. On 6 September 1980 recently ex-works No 50011** *Centurion* **coasts past Silverton, in the Exe Valley, at the head of the 07.50 Kensington Olympia–St Austell.** *Dave Mitchell*

Right: **Paddington–Oxford diagrams were covered for many years up to 1990. On 5 April 1980 No 50018** *Resolution* **takes the Didcot-avoiding line at the head of the 15.00 down service.** *David N. Clough*

A 'normal' Class 50 effort from July 1978 saw No 50023 (always a good performer) take 11 air-conditioned coaches to Reading in 28min 23sec. Top speed was 93, and the engine output 2,700bhp. Interestingly, in the same week No 50030 (another strong machine over its life) made a fractionally faster run between Hanwell and Twyford, with a 94mph maximum but with an extra coach. This was no fluke, because No 50021 (always a good bet for a fine run) matched No 50030 virtually to the second and was only five weeks off a light overhaul. It was therefore surprising that two runs with this machine established that its speedometer was over-recording by 5mph at 90mph.

A series of runs on the 'Cornish Riviera Express' and 'Golden Hind' in July 1978 demonstrate some of the factors that affect train running. The former did not stop until Taunton but was squeezed in amongst the evening commuter services that might only have 90mph rolling stock or a Class 47 as power; in consequence it had a couple of minutes' pathing allowance inserted before Reading and rarely got a clear run to there. Across the runs, between 1 and 3min were dropped to Southall due to signals, and that

was usually not the end of it. Route upgrading for HST operation now brought a series of permanent-way slacks in the Kennett Valley. Only on one run was the 90mph line limit seriously exceeded, and this was a 100mph dash down towards Edington.

Of four runs, two were on time by Castle Cary, one was still 5min down, and the fourth was caught behind the 16.48 Paddington–Exeter all-stations that was heavily delayed due to locomotive failure; by Taunton the defecit had become 18min. Climbing to Whiteball, No 50020 made the slowest exit from Taunton but easily the fastest ascent, with 76mph through Wellington and 65 at the top. This was an exceptional effort and may have been a factor in why the locomotive failed a few days later on the 16.48 down, as noted above. The other three climbs were unremarkable and were typical of the period. Such recordings confirm someone was derating the class; journeys made on the 'Golden Hind' in 1975 did not display such under-powering.

In the up direction, the 'Riviera' was timed to complete the Exeter–Paddington leg in 149min with a 10-car load. The

The WR was quick to deploy the new arrivals on non-passenger work. On 16 May 1974 – less than two weeks after the mass migration – No 50023 passes West Ealing with the Acton–St Erth milk tanks. *N. E. Preedy*

same stock was then turned around for the evening's 'Golden Hind'. There was the customary variation in driving style evident as far as Taunton. Some drivers sauntered out of St Davids station, whilst others drove properly and opened up quickly. Some sensibly allowed the gradient to pull speed down to the 75mph permitted between Hele and Cullompton, whilst others used the brakes. Finally, most kept power on descending Whiteball and so topped 90mph. A few coasted down to Taunton and so speed barely exceeded 80, although this was sufficient for timekeeping.

An Exeter driver explained that it was customary to drive a '50' down Wellington Bank but to allow a '47' to coast. This reflected the ride qualities round the reverse curves through Wellington, where the Brush Type 4 rolled but the EE design did not. Differences in driving style can easily mask the abilities of different locomotives when only speeds are used to form the comparison. It can also cancel out the handicap of a heavier load. Notwithstanding checks for track work and signals, all these runs on the up 'Riviera' were on time or early passing Southcote Junction, just before Reading.

Continuing to Paddington, the fastest speed was attained by the weakest locomotive on the heaviest load! No 50019's driver had realised that the speedometer was optimistic and so kept the power controller wide open. With 11 air-conditioned coaches, 97mph was averaged between Burnham and Hanwell, with a 98 maximum – but with 105 on the speedometer. On the other runs the drivers were killing time to avoid too early an arrival in London. It was interesting to have No 50021 in this direction. The power developed climbing Whiteball was 2,175rhp, and allowance then needs to be made for ETH for the air-conditioned stock. This calculation holds up well in comparison to the trip behind No 50030 out of Paddington, described earlier, when both made virtually the same times as far as Iver, where No 50021 was eased.

Really the Bristol road was where Class 50 should have been in its element. Loads of eight or nine coaches and (at worst) moderate gradients enabled running around the 100mph mark to be attained and sustained for miles. Three runs have been chosen from personal records to illustrate performance prior to 1980. One was made in 1977, when the

Another semi-regular freight job from 1975 was the transfer freight from Acton to Norwood Junction. Heading for home on 20 April 1978, No 50040 negotiates third-rail territory at Wandsworth Common.
David N. Clough collection

timetable was shared with HSTs; the second was in 1980 and made on HST timings, while the third was in 1978 on a Paddington–Worcester service, with a first stop at Swindon.

The Bristol trains comprised nine air-conditioned vehicles, with the train supply in use. No 50028 was handicapped by a very stiff headwind but nevertheless kept time. (Figures in brackets after running times are for the HST schedule.) From Paddington to Slough No 50011 took 15min 30sec (13), with 98mph at Iver – it was evident that the locomotive's speedometer was over-reading by 3mph. Forward to Reading occupied 14min 27sec (11), with a 97mph maximum. Continuing to Didcot, No 50028 took 15min 15sec, with a 91mph maximum; No 50011 was faster, in 13min 57sec (13), and just touched 100mph. No 50028 ran on to Swindon in 21min 25sec, but No 50011 cut this to 19min 29sec (18). Both runs caught a couple of checks before reaching Bristol which spoiled the running. Nevertheless, some sprightly averages had clearly been achieved between stops. Didcot–Swindon, at 24.15 miles, was the longest leg, and the averages here were 66.6 and 74.4mph respectively.

No 50033 had an eight-car air-conditioned consist on the 09.23 Paddington–Worcester. The start was sluggish with such a load, only 83mph being attained by Hanwell, after which signals cut speed to 30mph. Accelerating all the way from Southall to Twyford, the train passed the latter at 101mph, and the customary slowing to 80 through Reading was followed by a second maximum of 101 at Steventon. A check at Wantage Road to 55.5 meant that nothing better than 95mph could be regained on the steepening grades around Shrivenham. Swindon was reached in 56min 58sec, or 51min net (average 91mph). The schedule of 66min would have included 4min recovery time, but, even so, it shows how undemanding WR booked timings were for locomotive-hauled services, because No 50033 had gained 13min. The driver reported using full power throughout, except for the slacks.

How well were the three machines performing? No 50028 had not been shopped for nearly four years and, not surprisingly, was the weakest. Allowing for the strong headwind and the ETH load, it

was just about within normal parameters, at about 2,650bhp. Both the other two class members had been outshopped only a couple of months before the journeys in question. Very detailed analysis of No 50033 suggests that some technical problem impaired the initial acceleration to Hanwell, but calculations suggest 2,770bhp thereafter. During long spells at around 100mph the rail horsepower was still 2,050, before allowing for ETH. No 50011 was clearly incorrectly set up, because the power developed was the highest known personally in this direction and suggests 3,100bhp. Comparison of the times and speeds with No 50028 reveals a significant advantage to No 50011 – a standard never matched after refurbishment, when it was something of a dud.

Speediness was demonstrated by a run with No 50042, timed by Peter Rutter, before refurbishment. On an up service from Bristol with eight air-conditioned coaches, the driver seems to have used full controller from Reading. There were two maxima of 107mph, and Paddington was reached in 26min 28sec – a gain of 1½min on the net schedule. After refurbishment the same machine was timed by John Baxter but with an extra coach. Despite this the time to Twyford was 16sec faster than Mr Rutter's trip, and this difference was maintained to Maidenhead, which was passed at 103mph. Here the driver eased

By 1980 increasing encroachment by HSTs brought consideration to the use of pairs of Class 50s on double-length stone trains. On 3 March 1980 Nos 50021 *Rodney* and 50024 *Vanguard*, complete with test coach, handle a 3,300-ton train near Ufton Crossing *en route* from Witham to Acton. *D. E. Canning*

back, but this shows that No 50042's first run was not made by a locomotive in top fettle, because it was not as sprightly as after refurbishment. Publication of these logs in the Class 50 Society's magazine *The Hoover* brought a reminder to Old Oak Common drivers about adhering to the 100mph limit.

In July 1977 BR abandoned its long-standing ban on the application of new locomotive names. Significantly, the two classes selected for adornment were 87 and 50, the latter to be known as the 'Warships' by virtue of receiving Royal Navy names. Some of these had been used previously on the diesel-hydraulic Class 42 and 43 'Warships', and the class name never caught on with Class 50. Pride of the fleet No 50035 had the honour of being the first to be named, on 17 January 1978, receiving *Ark Royal* plates in a ceremony at Plymouth at which the aircraft carrier's captain presented replica ship's badges, to be carried above the nameplates. No 50048 *Dauntless* was next, on 16 March in a ceremony at Reading. No 50006 was the last and received its *Neptune* plates

whilst undergoing refurbishment in Doncaster Works; this was the only naming off the WR, and Laira sent the plates to Doncaster on 20 June 1979, with Production Manager Martin Pridmore doing the honours in September. No 50035 was not the only one to be twinned with the ship after which it was named, as eventually 12 Class 50s carried ships' badges; of these, No 50032 *Courageous* would be unique in having the background to its plates painted blue (instead of the customary red) for the presentation by the Royal Navy of replica badges, on 11 October 1986.

During late 1979 and early 1980 the class took part in trials in pairs on stone trains from Merehead Quarry, Somerset, to Acton. These were partly to evaluate the suitability of the type for such services, with double the usual load, and partly to evaluate the feasibility of running longer, heavier trains. Class 50 was selected because of its ability to work in multiple and also because the introduction from 1980 of HSTs on Paddington–West of England services would release a number

Heavy repairs at Old Oak Common involved lifting No 50048 off its bogies on 16 November 1974.
David Rapson

for alternative duties. Although the heavy-load trials did not immediately bear fruit, they formed the basis for acquisition by Foster Yeoman, with BR blessing, of the heavy-haul General Motors Class 59s.

HSTs began to appear on West of England diagrams early in 1980, and the full timetable was introduced from May. Yet again, however, technical problems forced the continued use of Class 50s, often on HST timings. It was the EE diesel – not its Brush Class 47 counterpart – that was generally called upon by the WR to deputise. Meanwhile, from late 1979, training of Waterloo, Salisbury and Exeter drivers began as part of the planned deployment of the class on the Waterloo–Exeter route, displacing Class 33s. This also took effect from the May 1980 timetable, 15min being cut from the end-to-end times. Appearances were not confined to the former LSWR main line, however, and No 50001 was probably the first to traverse

the Bournemouth line, being observed at Brockenhurst on 9 July 1980. On 11 October it seems also to have made a class debut on the Brighton–Exeter service.

On 28 January 1979 No 50003 was involved in a collision with the stock of the 21.30 Penzance–Paddington at Plymouth. The locomotive was coming onto the stock when a brake malfunction occurred, possibly due to frosty conditions. As a result, a modification was made to the operation of the brake system on all Class 50s. No 50003 did not emerge from Doncaster for 18 months, and during this interval it was refurbished. Although scheduled to be the second in that programme, this proved not to be the case, because it took the works longer to allocate time to the cab rebuild.

By 1981 the allocation was again split between three depots: Laira had 34, Old Oak Common 10, while Bath Road still clung to six (Nos 50039-44).

A pay agreement at Bath Road saw a bonus paid, based on locomotive availability. Arrival of Class 50, with a difficult settling-in period, strained relations, because the prospects for a bonus nosedived. When this picture was taken in 1973 only Nos 400/1 were based on the WR, at Bath Road; both are receiving unclassified repairs on shed. *Philip D. Hawkins*

Right: **Cornwall witnessed Class 50 operation from May 1974. No 50028 is pictured at St Austell with the 1A69 08.35 Penzance–Paddington on 20 September 1974.**
David Rapson

Below: **Nameplate style, with lettering in polished metal on a red background. No 50002 *Superb* was one of the first to be twinned with its RN namesake.**
David N. Clough

Below right: **After Nos 50002/8/ 35/50 had been twinned, BR specified that future replica ships' badges had to be smaller, as demonstrated by No 50044. Sometimes the badges were mounted above the nameplate, sometimes below, and the position sometimes changed following a repaint.**
David N. Clough

Left: **Booked pairings were common, notably on summer Sundays. On 6 June 1982 un-refurbished No 50046** *Ajax* **heads refurbished No 50048** *Dauntless* **on the 14.40 Sundays-only Plymouth–Paddington at Brewham.**
John Chalcraft

Below: **No 50014 passes Tiverton Junction with the 1V90 13.21 Liverpool–Plymouth on 16 September 1974.**
David Rapson

Right: **Having arrived at Bristol Temple Meads on a service from Paddington, No 50037 passes Victoria Park, Bedminster, with empty stock bound for Malago Vale carriage sidings on 5 June 1974.**
David Rapson

Below: **A rather travel-stained No 50032 passes Tiverton Junction at the head of a down service on 5 July 1975.**
David Rapson

Below right: **Late in the afternoon of 2 September 1978, No 50049 *Defiance* emerges from Whiteball Tunnel with a Paddington–Plymouth parcels.**
John Chalcraft

Left: **When headcode numbers were dispensed with, some class members unofficially received all or part of their number on the plated-over space. Carrying '05', No 50005** *Collingwood* **shuffles up the slow line at Goring with an up freight on 19 May 1979.** *John Chalcraft*

Below: **No 50026** *Indomitable* **shunts milk tanks at Lostwithiel as part of the 16.42 St Erth– Clapham service on 26 June 1979.** *John Chalcraft*

Above: **Cornish freight turns were used by Laira for locomotives deemed unfit for passenger duty for a variety of reasons. On 25 June 1979 No 50037 stands at St Blazey, having arrived from Tavistock Junction on a combined engineers' and cement train.** *John Chalcraft*

Right: **No 50018** *Resolution* **at Exeter St Davids on 14 May 1982.** *Dave Mitchell*

Below right: **Until Sectorisation, Class 50s were staple power for the overnight trains between Paddington and the West Country. No 50014** *Warspite* **has just arrived at Paddington with the 20.45 from Penzance on 21 July 1981.** *David N. Clough*

6 *Refurbishment*

It is clear that there was a difference in philosophy between the LMR and WR. The latter declined offers of help from the former during the period post reallocation in 1974 and was less tolerant of a number of the distinctive features built into the class. Part of the explanation may lie in the fact that the WR regarded the Class 50s as passenger locomotives, whereas they were very much mixed-traffic workhorses when allocated to Crewe. On-line failures were disruptive – especially so once the HSTs had arrived, because these could not easily be used to propel a beleaguered '50'-hauled service out of the way. John Butt, then Locomotive Engineer, WR, told

the SPWG meeting of 14 March 1977 that the poor level of reliability had to be improved. It was at this meeting that the idea was first floated of a partial rebuild to eradicate as many as possible of the factors that caused trouble.

The WR had every reason to seek a long-term solution to the reliability issues, because the class was to form an integral part of its motive-power fleet for many years. Despite counter-arguments from the LMR, the WR began isolating equipment that it deemed superfluous, in an attempt to reduce depot time needed to find faults. The dynamic-braking equipment was among the first, following a trial (involving

Seen during refurbishment at Doncaster in August 1982, No 50024 *Vanguard* has had all its equipment removed and its bodywork prepared and primed. In front is a discarded inertial-filter unit. *David N. Clough*

85

10 Bath Road locomotives) staged to assess the savings in brake-block wear by retention of the system. This was investigated during 1974, following an incident in which a tyre was fractured, and suspicion fell on the way the dynamic brake operated. Peter Fox, then a metallurgist with BR, carried out the research that involved isolation of the equipment on four machines (Nos 50012/3/32/46). It was concluded that, provided depot staff set up the system properly, it worked very well.

The results of the Bath Road trial were reported on 11 December 1975 to the SPWG and led the WR to believe the cost of maintenance to be greater than the savings in brake-gear wear. At the same meeting other electronic systems were proposed for isolation. The Class 50's closed-loop control system was a sensible design and offered the opportunity to employ sub-systems for dynamic braking, high and low wheelslip protection, tractive-effort control and slow-speed operation. However, a problem with any one of these sub-systems necessitated a detailed check of the entire closed loop, to identify the fault. Removing a sub-system from the closed loop meant that it could not cause a problem, so fault-finding was quicker. One result of the removal of dynamic braking was more frequent attention to bogie brake gear. As an economy measure during construction, the class had not been fitted with automatic slack-adjusters on the bogies, it being assumed that the dynamic-braking system would lessen the use of the friction brakes. However, brake adjustment was not easy and absorbed much depot time, and eventually the WR obtained sanction to fit automatic slack-adjusters experimentally to one member of the class.

Another issue which continued to plague the class was that of air management. Clogged inertial filters could be detected by a change in the sound made by the locomotives. Some, like No 50041 during 1978, barely emitted a whine, because the filter mazes had accumulated such a build-up of dirt. Presumably unofficially, Laira tried to remove this grime by resorting to drastic measures. The filters in No 50026 were removed to an isolated spot on the depot, doused with paraffin and set alight. This proved disastrous, however, because the fine-steel filter-fins warped, and the unit would not re-seat into an air-tight position within the locomotive. The grime remained *in situ*.

Technology had moved on since the Class 50 control circuitry had been designed and built in the mid-1960s. Repeated removal of the KV10 field-supply units, due to failure, had caused problems with the connections. In fact, in October 1974 these components were described as life-expired, and consideration was being given to their replacement, together with other items of electronics. A report dated 12 July 1977 proposed many of the modifications to the control cubicle that eventually became part of the refurbishment programme, and by September 1978 a rationalised CU1 (the 'brain' of the control system), with sub-systems such as tractive-effort control, slow-speed control and dynamic braking eliminated, was being trialled in No 50016.

A further factor that influenced the decision to bundle all the changes together was the time it took to get modifications approved through the BRB. It seems that a revision of procedures following the Ealing derailment in December 1973 meant that it could take a year to get Board approval. What came to be called the 'refurbishment programme' was an attempt to improve reliability by a significant degree, in a way not possible by piecemeal measures. There is no better illustration of why such drastic measures were needed than the availability and reliability figures for 1977 and 1978:

	Availability (%)	Reliability (mpc)
1977	70	13,872
1978	63	8,314

Doncaster Works was not helping the availability position, because of the shortage of repaired major components. Whereas in June 1977 only five machines were present, by June 1978 the figure had risen to 11 (22%) and remained around that number until the end of the year. The WR had based its availability targets on the assumption that only two locomotives would be in works at any one time, but in order to run a realistic service it had to revise this: for planning purposes in 1979 only 55% would be diagrammed for traffic. However, something had to be done to address worsening reliability, and this would then result in higher availability. Additionally, servicing costs would be reduced – another prime objective, because the class was proving extremely expensive when compared with other Type 4s.

BR's Railway Technical Centre (RTC) at Derby drew up plans to reflect changes that the WR deemed necessary, and BREL assessed how much the work would cost. Eventually agreement was reached and BRB approval received for a general overhaul (previously, overhauls had been classified as 'light' or 'intermediate') and refurbishment. Although the WR had

A simplified set of instruments was adopted as part of the refurbishment programme. Note the difference from the cab desk as built, depicted on page 18.
David N. Clough

Doncaster Works was responsible for Class 50 overhauls from January 1977 until March 1987. Complete with its unique all-blue roof, No 50010 (minus *Monarch* nameplates) receives an intermediate overhaul on 23 March 1985 – the last time it was 'shopped'. *David N. Clough*

requested replacement of the troublesome main generator with an alternator, this was ruled out on cost grounds; in short, the class was not deemed worth the money – a short-sighted decision. Nevertheless, the scope of the work sanctioned meant that the end product was virtually a new locomotive at one quarter of the cost of a new build.

The RTC Locomotive Drawing Office at Derby carried out detailed design work but found a general lack of information about the class within BR. This was a consequence of the earlier hire arrangement between BR and EE. When the locomotives were on hire BR had no need for detailed manufacturing drawings, and by the time they were bought by BR provision of the detailed drawings was lost in the 'noise' of the deal. Doncaster Works admitted the '50s' had provided something of a challenge, the more so when the refurbishment programme commenced.

Whilst the basic modification design had been done at Derby, it soon became

apparent that, because of slight build differences between each locomotive and as a result of an uncontrolled Regional modification programme, a degree of 'site engineering' would be needed to produce a final design. At that time there was an outpost of the RTC drawing office based at Doncaster, to cover local work packages and provide technical support to the works. (Similar teams existed at other works.) From within this outpost Frank Alcock was appointed as Class 50 Project Engineer and started to co-ordinate the works' feedback and queries with the specialists back at the RTC and the Regional technical staff. The Works had appointed Martin Pridmore as Project Manager and the Regional representative was an ex-Laira technical assistant, David Shillito. To be fair, once the new team and the works staff got to grips with the idiosyncrasies of the type, they demonstrated an ability to deliver a quality product that only rarely needed rectification.

THE WORK IN DETAIL

A 'General & Refurbish' overhaul (GRF) comprised four main aspects. First, there was the removal of redundant equipment. Second, there was the need to provide an effective air-management system. Third, a full refurbishment and rehabilitation of the electronics and electrical machines was carried out, together with technical updating. Finally, there was the general overhaul work normally carried out on BR traction on a 12-yearly cycle, involving complete overhaul of all major components.

On arrival at Doncaster, a locomotive was stripped and cleaned, with the bodywork stripped of all paint to reveal rust that would require removal and possibly bodyside re-plating. A coat of primer was then applied before bodywork attention was carried out. The roof at No 2 end was re-plated where previously there had been a recess for the vents for the dynamic-brake resistance bank, because these were no longer required. Bodyside sand-fillers were plated over, and the sand boxes and pipework removed. Pipework for the weight-transfer-compensation equipment was also discarded. The train-headcode panels, redundant for several years were blanked off, and two fixed marker lights fitted in lieu. A window in the engine room was replaced by a grille as part of the modified air-management scheme. Provision was made in the cab front to fit a centre headlight.

Discarded equipment comprised both sets of inertial filters, the associated pressurising fan and motor and the dynamic-brake resistances. A revised CU1 control unit had the slow-speed and tractive-effort controls and low-speed-wheelslip-protection and dynamic-braking sub-systems eliminated. Redundant cab instrumentation was also dispensed with. High-speed wheelslip-protection and the anti-slip brake were retained, and a revised instrument panel for the driver was installed which provided better illumination, in keeping with the general BR modification to add a perspex scale into each instrument.

Removal of the dynamic-brake resistances created space for alternative air filters. These were of the same type as fitted to Class 56 and HST power cars. In fact, No 2 end was radically different and altogether more airy than before – and also considerably cleaner. The large inertial-filter unit and resistance bank had gone, replaced on one side by a bank of filters, drawing air in through the bodyside louvres that had previously cooled the resistances. A roof-level extractor fan in the engine room was supposed to scavenge

Whilst the refurbishment programme was in progress, several class members received intermediate overhauls, because they could not be spared long enough for the general overhaul to be done. One such was No 50014 *Warspite*, seen departing Doncaster on a trial run to Tyne Yard on 9 April 1980. *John E. Oxley*

air. In practice, it frequently became clogged with deposits from the engine-room environment and seized in consequence – truly an ineffective arrangement. Externally it was topped by what looked like a Chinaman's hat. Some have argued that the air management post refurbishment was still not ideal, but a cleaner locomotive interior was produced. A fresh bulkhead was fitted to separate the engine room from the generator compartment, seated across the main generator. This was one of the local changes to the RTC design, in that the outer parts containing the doors and door frames were made fixed, only the inner section being removable, to allow the engine-and-generator set to be taken out; this ensured that the door arrangement and integrity could be maintained by a more permanent installation.

EE was involved in the repair and refurbishment of various components, notably being contracted to carry out a full rewind of the main-generator armature to address the result of years of ingress of oil and dirt caused by poor air management and leaks from adjacent components. Doncaster carried out rehabilitation of the main-generator carcase and traction motors. Where necessary the traction motors were also rewound. A further original design fault requiring rectification was the routeing of power cables at floor level, because they suffered from attack by oil and dirt, which caused the insulation to break down. Spurious electrical signals could then result and affect the performance of the sensitive electronic equipment. These faults were a nightmare for depot staff to trace and remedy. Refurbishment brought full rewiring and the siting of the conduit trunking along the bodyside and away from the floor.

Works personnel rewired the control cubicle using wiring diagrams produced by the RTC. The modified CU1 trialled in No 50016 became the standard and in October 1978 was fitted in No 50006, the latter becoming the prototype refurbished machine. Sent to works on 21 September 1977 for a main-generator change, it had languished for a year before being selected for modification. Updating of the electronics, including the KV10 units, also took place.

Other changes undertaken at the time included fitting a larger underframe tank to collect engine-room spillage, while four-part brushes replaced two-part ones on the main generator, to aid commutation, and a slightly higher-pressure piston-scraper ring was adopted to reduce the amount of oil passing into the combustion chamber and finding its way into the exhaust system. Engine running-in after overhaul was done as quickly as possible as a result of experience with No 50047: its engine was left idling for long periods while being set up after rebuild, causing the cylinder liners to glaze; oil-throwing after return to service became obvious, and the locomotive was sent back to Doncaster for an engine change.

Most obvious of all the refurbishment revisions was the application of a new livery, starting with the seventh member of the programme. No 50023 received all-yellow cabs, with black window surrounds and a BR double-arrow logo that extended from cantrail to solebar. Initially the bodyside numbers were small on this progenitor of the livery, but this was soon changed to the familiar large type.

No 50006 was subjected to extensive tests on works. These included static checks prior to a load test in the test house, whereby the traction motors are disconnected and replaced by resistor units that can be varied to simulate a loaded train. No 50006 was connected up and the engine started. It is normal for EE engines to 'hunt' up and down the rev range when first started from cold, but that in No 50006 was exceptional in the way it surged alarmingly up and down the scale. Clearly something was amiss, but hours of investigation revealed nothing. Finally Terry Almond, one of the test fitters, arrived with two gate valves which he proceeded to connect in the hydraulic load-regulator hoses that fed the vane motor in the generator-excitation circuit. By progressively restricting these valves Terry managed to get 2,700hp to behave itself to permit engine running-in as quickly as possible, so that the cylinder liners did not become glazed. It wasn't until the next day that investigations concluded that the new load-control system was quicker in its reaction time than the original and so required some damping. This was later incorporated in the form of chokes in the hose union connections.

The initial load test resulted in running for a period at up to 117% of normal

Above: Following refurbishment, No 50049 *Defiance* was routed via the York-avoiding line as part of its trial run on 10 June 1982. *David N. Clough*

Left: Latterly the ER seemed to prefer running works trial trains south along the ECML instead of north to the Newcastle area. No 50005 *Collingwood* sets off for Peterborough on 22 March 1986. Note the contrast in cleanliness between the locomotive and its train. *Les Nixon*

maximum output (3,160bhp). Frank Alcock reported that the main generator sparked like a Catherine wheel and eventually flashed over so badly that it needed to be changed. Otherwise the refurbishment was satisfactory. No 50006 was returned to traffic on 14 November 1979, having been sidelined for longer than any other Class 50. Livery was the standard BR blue, and this was the pattern for Nos 50001/13/7/9/47, which would not receive the revised, 'large logo' livery until the next classified overhaul. No 50017 also retained its bodyside sand fillers until next overhaul – the only refurbished example to do so. It also had the distinction of being the last to carry the BR emblems under the driver's cab windows; c1974 the position of these had been moved to the centre of the bodyside, but, after naming, the location changed again to under the secondman's cabside window.

Following the problems with No 50006 came those with No 50047. Over the years Doncaster's original two-berth test house had been extended to include an adjacent soundproofed booth that accommodated another two locomotives. No 50047 was duly connected to one of these positions, and engine running-in commenced. After a couple of hours a smell of burning varnish

was becoming apparent, and the generator body was getting hot to touch, but the locomotive nevertheless continued to give the required output. Eventually things got so bad that the test had to be stopped for investigation. Close examination revealed that an additional plate had been fitted in the generator-fan casing by a WR depot, effectively blanking-off the outlet. Once this was removed the temperatures stabilised, and the machine cooled down.

The customary trial run to Newcastle and back on a test rake allowed for shakedown issues to be identified. No 50025 seems to hold the record for the number of trial trips, with a total of nine due to power-unit problems. Although a BRB inspector accompanied these runs on behalf of the WR, the latter carried out a full technical audit of each locomotive on arrival back on Region. One or two were sent for rectification, whilst No 50025 was judged not to be ideal and had its power unit derated slightly at Old Oak Common, its home depot. Once procedures had become established, Doncaster was able to carry out a GRF repair in 95 days – a most creditable achievement. However, with the programme already underway, the WR needed to have several class members overhauled quickly, and these received an

When the intermediate overhaul of No 50035 *Ark Royal* was completed in July 1986, Doncaster did not have the requisite paint for Network SouthEast livery, so the locomotive returned to the WR in grey primer. It is seen arriving at Doncaster on the 1D21 12.45 Peterborough–Doncaster test train on 12 July. *David Rapson*

The ER borrowed No 50009 for the 08.30 Leeds–King's Cross on 16 June 1977. The locomotive was the first to be overhauled at Doncaster and was a surprise visitor to Potters Bar, where this picture was taken. *J. Rickard*

intermediate. Nos 50011/27 were the last to be dealt with in this way and so became among the last to be refurbished.

By 1981 it was possible to compare the reliability of refurbished and un-refurbished examples. Whilst the latter had improved to a reasonable 10,263mpc – similar to the figure achieved by the WR's Class 47/4s – the former managed an average for the year of 16,855mpc, against a target of 15,000mpc. Of course, locomotives recently put through such a radical overhaul ought to have been more reliable.

Even during the 'honeymoon' year of 1981, availability of the refurbished examples averaged just 76.5%, and by 1983 this had dropped to 63.6%. Lest the improvement in the 1981 performance figures be seen as too praiseworthy, it is instructive to remember those quoted in the previous chapter for the remaining 14 LMR allocation, which achieved 76.9% availability and 26,252mpc between May 1975 and January 1976. Nevertheless, the WR had got a nearly new locomotive for about 25% of the cost of a brand-new one.

One is left wondering whether the once-and-for-all improvement in reliability was truly achieved for a sustained period. Countering this, of course, the un-refurbished locomotives would have become steadily less reliable; indeed, the SR quickly demanded that only refurbished machines operate over its metals on the Waterloo–Exeter route. It was also envisaged that the Class 50s would last only until 1994, by which time they would be due a further general overhaul, on average 12 years after the previous one.

The refurbishment programme was completed in 1983. No 50002 was sent to works because it was throwing oil, being followed by No 50030 after the latter suffered a main-generator failure, leaving just one un-refurbished machine. No 50014 was still performing well when it entered Doncaster on 23 May 1983. It was released on 7 December but, as explained in the next chapter, became one of the first withdrawals, four years later almost to the day.

Isolation and removal of the dynamic brake had a downside. Talk to LMR staff

and they will tell you how a '50' could stop on a sixpence, so effective was the dynamic brake. No one thought to consider how the locomotive's braking curve would be affected by not having this equipment in use. The WR found out when several instances occurred of Class 50s overrunning red signals when hauling short newspaper trains. (With longer trains, the rolling stock provided sufficient braking effort to compensate.) As a precaution to avoid further signal overruns, the WR reduced the maximum speed to 95mph with effect from 1 November 1982.

The subsequent investigation into the newspaper-train incidents revealed that the vans were prone to being overloaded with dense newsprint and that this had the effect of distorting the train's braking performance. Individually the vehicles complied with the requirements of the BR braking curve, but only at their rated loadings. The solution was to add more vehicles to the newspaper trains.

After exactly a year the WR reintroduced the 100mph limit. This was said to be to allow other Regions to make use of the higher speed, but, in truth, at that time the class was not used on any routes off the WR where 100mph was permitted.

A side-effect of refurbishment was the removal of non-standard fitments. For example, No 50015 had run with two-speed windscreen wipers on the driver's side, and these reverted to standard. No 50011 carried the digits '11' in the centre of the headcode box at No 2 end. As the programme progressed, one or two modifications crept in to recreate prototype features on trial. No 50007 was released with a revised CU4, which reintroduced the facility for the radiator fan not to turn unless the engine required cooling. Although this had been a feature as built, at some time it had been removed, which had meant the fan always turned.

Laira machines destined for works occasionally hauled a cross-country service to Leeds or York, but usually the locomotive was not a runner. The most common method of transfer was as freight from Tavistock Junction to Severn Tunnel Junction, with onward transit in a Doncaster-bound service. For Old Oak Common examples, a trip across London to Temple Mills was followed by inclusion in a freight, first to March and then to Doncaster. From the Winter 1980 timetable until May 1982 the 09.50 Edinburgh–Plymouth, which changed traction at York, was the most common route home for a Laira machine; thereafter the 17.35 Leeds–Bristol, the 12.37 Leeds–Cardiff or the Penzance 09.23 Newcastle–Plymouth were used. Some Old Oak Common '50s' ran up the ECML, rather than heading across country.

Run-down to Retirement

Until the sectorisation on BR in the late 1980s, life for the Class 50s was pretty much as it had been since 1980. By then, the class was active on the Waterloo–Exeter route, after being largely displaced from most West of England duties by HSTs. The arrival of the latter on the cross-country trains from Penzance and Plymouth to the North and Scotland had little impact, because generally the '50s' were used only on workings that changed traction at Birmingham, whereas the HSTs tended to operate diagrams to Sheffield, Leeds, York and beyond.

A good indication of where the class could be found can be gleaned from the following list of stabling points during the July 1982 ASLEF strike: Laira (14), Old Oak Common (15), Bath Road (2), Saltley (1), Reading (1), Oxford (1), Gloucester (1), Hereford (1), Salisbury (2), Exeter (4), Stewarts Lane (2) and Doncaster (6). In addition to those in works, 16 (including No 50022 at Reading) were stopped for maintenance or repair. The number out of service probably reflects the opportunity taken (by virtue of the strike) to carry out major work on depot.

Driver training at Saltley during early 1981, using No 50027, brought some unusual workings, especially overnight. For example, having arrived in Birmingham on the 19.00 ex Paddington, the '50' would take a parcels train from Curzon Street to Peterborough and then one back to Leicester. From here it ran light to Nuneaton to collect a Parkstone Quay–Lawley Street Freightliner before returning home on the 09.20 Manchester Piccadilly–Poole between Birmingham and

Displacement from West of England expresses by HSTs meant the class could be seen more extensively on other routes. On 16 November 1982 No 50041 *Bulwark* approaches Banbury with the 10.34 Manchester Piccadilly–Paddington, which it had taken over at Birmingham. This shot illustrates well the post-refurbishment 'large logo' paint scheme. *Alex Dasi-Sutton*

No 50043 *Eagle* departs
Cheltenham with the 09.35
Liverpool–Penzance on
14 March 1985. *John Chalcraft*

Reading. Appearances north of Birmingham on daytime passenger services also increased. Such forays could be as far as York – possibly the limit of Saltley drivers' route knowledge.

By the start of 1982 the class was split between Laira and Old Oak Common, the latter having Nos 50028-38/48. After Old Oak Common lost some Class 31s it took additional Class 50s from Laira and by January 1983 had Nos 50021-40.

From May 1983 there were 34 turns, Mondays to Fridays. These involved passenger train movements from Paddington to Thames Valley destinations, (including Newbury and Westbury), Bristol, Birmingham, Hereford and Plymouth. In addition there were several diagrams from Plymouth to Birmingham, with Class 2 services in Cornwall and between Bristol

and Taunton also being covered. The Waterloo route required six locomotives. Use on Class 3 parcels and a couple of freights in the Exeter area rounds off the picture, Paddington–Cheltenham services having gone over to HSTs from the Summer 1982 timetable.

Further driver training, this time at Cardiff Canton, was clearly aimed at broadening the class's sphere of operation in the light of displacement by HSTs; No 50045 seems to have been the first to be used. Later the class began to work regularly to Swansea. With the number of locomotives at Doncaster much reduced as the refurbishment programme came to an end, the number of Class 50 diagrams rose to 36 (72%) from the Winter 1983 timetable.

Stabling of a Class 50 overnight at Hereford sometimes brought unexpected nocturnal duties and probably explains how No 50014 came to be in charge of the 03.20 Carlisle–Severn Tunnel Junction freight on 13 February 1981, although just where it took over the train, which normally changed motive power at Crewe, is not known. A new diagram was assigned on 24 January 1983, which started with the 1S39 07.35 Plymouth–Glasgow as far as Birmingham New Street; No 50008 had the honour of taking the first train.

During 1983 persistent rumours circulated that Class 50s were to be reallocated to the ER, which by then had lost its Class 55 'Deltics'. History proved these stories to be groundless, though it might have happened, had East Coast electrification been sanctioned only as far as Newcastle; pairs of Class 50s would then have been used northwards. Perhaps the most memorable event of 1983 was the dreadful derailment of No 50041 outside Paddington in the early hours of 23 November. It had brought the up sleeper (21.35 ex Penzance and load 13) without incident until it was derailed at speed due to driver error. Miraculously there were no fatalities, and the engine was still running as No 50041 lay on its side. Damage to the locomotive was described as cosmetic, and it was duly despatched to Doncaster for repair and an intermediate overhaul.

The class was never free of problems for long, and in April 1984 underframe fractures at one end of the engine were observed on No 50022 during a routine internal washout at Old Oak Common. The existence of fractures was easily spotted because water cascaded out of the interior in places it shouldn't have and never had before! Examination revealed half the class to be affected. As far as possible, repairs were held over until the next classified repair at Doncaster, but where cracks were bigger than 3in a swift visit to works was deemed essential. On 5 August 1986, when No 50035 returned to Doncaster after an intermediate overhaul for camshaft repairs, underframe fractures were found at the other end of the engine room from those found initially. This was by no means a unique occurrence, and the WR carried out repairs itself.

A spate of main-generator failures in 1983 was the main cause of the poor availability described in Chapter 6.

Doncaster had no overhauled units to hand, and locomotives stood idle until a substitute became available. Some changes were done on works and some at Laira. This brought to light that not all the class had received a reconditioned main generator during refurbishment. Sanction to fit an alternator as a replacement in one example of the class was rejected by the BRB. Meanwhile, withdrawal of Class 40s at Doncaster brought a decision to reuse some of their engine blocks within the Class 50 pool.

Paintwork deteriorated quickly, and many machines presented a shabby appearance. The WR blamed Doncaster for poor paint adhesion, whereupon the works countered by telling the Region not to pour 'paintstripper' (*i.e.* chemicals used in washing plants) over its nice paintwork!

Haulage of the Glasgow Central–Cardiff service south of Birmingham brought Class 50s to the route through Chepstow. In charge of the 08.10 from Cardiff, No 50016 *Barham* crosses the River Wye on 25 May 1984. *John Chalcraft*

Above: **The 09.24 Paignton–Birmingham New Street and return worked a circular route to avoid running round. No 50029 *Renown* approaches Bournville on the return on 17 August 1985.** *David N. Clough*

Right: **Class 50 to the rescue! In post-refurbishment all-over blue, No 50047 *Swiftsure* assists Class 45 No 45051 down Ashley Down Bank with a late-running Manchester–Plymouth train in wintry conditions on 12 December 1981.** *John Chalcraft*

Grey for the roof, whilst smart when newly applied, was hardly a practical choice, because it soon became dirty with exhaust emissions. The WR sought BRB sanction to try black instead. Then in the summer of 1983 Landore repainted No 50010 and had no grey paint, so it used blue instead.

Doncaster offered a turnaround of seven weeks for an intermediate overhaul, and the WR planned 11 of these during 1984. Nos 50006/17/9/22 had already been sent for their first post-refurbishment classified repair. Generally, the plan to only have two machines undergoing classified work at one time was managed. The works also had to deal with at least one example at a time for underframe fractures. When No 50040 was sent for a trial run to Peterborough in July 1985 after classified overhaul and underframe fracture repairs, it sported *Glorious* nameplates, the works foreman having collected the wrong set of plates from the paintshop! No 50040, incidentally, had been in Doncaster for only 52 days – well inside the 11-week turnaround for classified overhaul.

Controversially among some enthusiasts, the WR renamed No 50007 from *Hercules* to *Sir Edward Elgar*. The ceremony to mark the renaming was held on 25 February 1984 – two days after the 50th anniversary of the composer's death. It received GWR Brunswick-green bodysides and a black roof, together with brass nameplates in GWR style. Several subsequent repaints varied slightly the shade of green, but the basic livery has been retained to this day. At the ceremony the WR's General Manager said more renamings would follow as part of the GWR150 celebrations in 1985, but this never happened.

Embarrassingly, No 50007's No 1 traction motor failed at Royal Oak on its inaugural run after the ceremony at Paddington, the 12.15 to Oxford, and it limped there and back on four motors. This was because the series/parallel motor configuration means that traction motors can be isolated only in pairs, rendering field-weakening inoperative. *En route* from Laira for the ceremony, No 4 motor (the other one in the pair with No 1) had failed

and been replaced at Old Oak Common. Planned use that evening to Hereford, via Worcester and Sir Edward's birthplace, was scuppered.

A feature of the May 1984 timetable was more loco-hauled services between Paddington and the West of England. These comprised two 'jumbo' workings of up to 14 vehicles and reversion of the 'Torbay Express', destination Paignton, to hauled stock. All were entrusted to Class 50s, but, in true WR style, the timings of the 'jumbos' were slothful. Better availability and some capacity in diagramming led to the class's appearing on excursion trains – virtually unknown on the LMR until after May 1974 and unusual on the WR before the early 1980s. Indeed, during August 1985 availability reached 90%. This permitted use on out-of-course passenger turns: on 5 June 1985 No 50027 appeared at Southampton Docks to haul a boat train to Waterloo, whilst the next day Nos 50039 and 50047 took Saga specials

from Newquay to Newcastle and Penzance to Paddington respectively. The LMR, meanwhile, became more adventurous in borrowing a spare '50' when one was on its territory. Hence Sunday 'drags' in the Birmingham/Nuneaton/Rugby area were not unusual, whilst forays between Wolverhampton and Shrewsbury on through services from Euston broke new ground. Mention must also be made of appearances on the 20.00 Morris Cowley–Harwich Parkeston Quay cars, an example being No 50048 on 12 June. The Winter 1985 diagrams required only 68% availability and included seven freight jobs; clearly work for the class was reducing.

The most interesting trip of 1985 was probably that undertaken by No 50030, which on 25 August worked F&W Railtours' Plymouth–Edinburgh charter run in conjunction with the Haymarket open day, in so doing making a class debut north of Newcastle. Although there were rumours of a twinning ceremony with nuclear submarine HMS *Repulse*, this did not happen, although No 50008 was re-dedicated to HMS *Thunderer* at Plymouth; repainted in 'large logo' colours but with a black roof, it was probably the first to gain red buffer-beams within this livery style. No 50046 was also twinned, with HMS *Ajax*, and acquired the same Laira variant of standard Class 50 livery as No 50008.

On the subject of liveries, with effect from No 50021, outshopped from Doncaster on 20 December 1985, an orange line was added around the body at roof level. Interestingly, this machine did not return home until 3 January 1986, powering the 20.22 Doncaster Belmont–Severn Tunnel Junction Speedlink freight. Nos 50040/3 acquired '40' and '43' respectively in the centre of No 2 end headcode box courtesy of a leading light in Class 50 preservation, whilst No 50019 also received similar treatment but with its full number. In 1986 No 50010 ran with 'D410' in its route-indicator box.

From April 1986 the overhaul policy changed as the concept of the 'F' exam began to be applied to Class 50. Instead of sending locomotives to works for classified repair, depots designated as Level 5 began to carry out 'F' exams, which involved the exchange of major components and fitting overhauled equipment supplied from a BREL workshop. Certain additional maintenance beyond the standard of an 'E' exam was also carried out, plus a repaint. Laira received Level 5 status for Class 50 work. During the 1986/7 financial year six 'F' exams were to be carried out at Laira, and six classified overhauls at Doncaster. Laira could deal with any Old Oak Common-based locomotive that fell due for

A dramatic sea-wall shot of No 50031 *Hood* passing Teignmouth with an up train on 30 September 1987.
David Rapson

overhaul; whether a unit went to Doncaster or Laira would depend on whether underframe fractures also needed repair, in which case the former would do the work.

The class's general high levels of reliability and utilisation during this period are apparent from the following. Selected at random, in February 1986 No 50019 covered 8,348 miles without any failures. Laira carried out a 'D' exam, but this was the only major maintenance needed. Duties covered were predominantly on the Waterloo line but also included quite a few trips to Paddington and to Penzance. There were no visits to Birmingham or South Wales. Only two changes of brake blocks were needed – a point that will be of significance later. Also worthy of mention is the class's nocturnal activity over the North & West route; No 50028 seems to hold the honour of putting in the first appearance, on the 20.00 Cardiff–Crewe on 4 November 1985.

Early in June 1986, in a portent of things to come, Nos 50017 and 50023 were repainted (at Laira and Old Oak Common respectively) in the new Network SouthEast (NSE) livery of red, white and blue. Sectorisation of BR was on the way, and with it, eventual privatisation. No 50023 took a Waterloo–Salisbury special on 10 June 1986 to launch NSE. Doncaster was unprepared for the revised livery, so when Old Oak Common-based No 50035 came off works on 14 July, it was still in grey primer, because the appropriate paint was not to hand. The following day it took the 09.35 Newcastle–Penzance from Sheffield to Bristol before proceeding to home base for final painting. It had undergone a classified overhaul after an extended period in traffic that exceeded 11,000 TOPS hours. This had been as an experiment, whereby Old Oak Common had carried out a 'Super E' exam, including full piston change, at the normal works shopping interval. In the event, the cost of the 'Super E' did not justify the extension of time between overhauls, and the policy was abandoned. During the period after the 'Super E' until shopping in 1986 the engine was derated slightly.

PERFORMANCE EXPLOITS

During the 1980s observers began to notice that certain locomotives were producing

some remarkable performances, of a standard never seen previously on a regular basis.

On 2 July 1985 No 50010 arrived at Exeter St Davids with the 09.21 Penzance–Paddington 'jumbo', loaded to 505 tons gross. From passing Cowley Bridge Junction in 2min 32sec at 47mph until clearing Whiteball in 18min 20sec at 66mph, the driver used full power and attained a maximum of 78 at Cullompton. This effort meant over 1½min had been gained already. Uninhibited driving saw the train hurtle through Wellington at 101mph, and a further minute was gained by Taunton. From 78.5mph passing Castle Cary, speed gradually fell to 61mph over Brewham. Recovering from a signal check to 43 at Heywood Road Junction meant the climb to Patney could not be rushed, but the minimum was 74, with 79mph over Savernake. To round off the effort, there was sustained running around the 100 mark between Thatcham and Theale. The

Top: For a couple of years in the mid-1980s, to relieve congestion on HSTs, the WR timetabled 'jumbo' (13-coach) loco-hauled services between Paddington and the West Country. On 6 August 1985 No 50017 *Royal Oak* carefully negotiates Newton Abbot with the 09.32 from Penzance. *David N. Clough*

Above: Cornish viaducts provide excellent photo opportunities. Moorswater is the setting for No 50018 *Resolution* and the 16.35 Plymouth–Penzance on 22 August 1986, at which time the class had custody of most local services between these towns. *David N. Clough*

net time from Exeter was 102½min (average speed 80.5mph), compared to a schedule (net of recovery time) of 115min – a gain to the locomotive of 12½min.

Continuing to Paddington, No 50010 reached a top speed of 97mph at Slough, and the average from Burnham to West Ealing was 95. Since the last two locations are at virtually the same height above sea level, this meant the balancing speed on level track was probably also 95. The time from Reading was 28min 24sec, showing a further gain of 1½min. With the aid of unused recovery time in the schedule, added to the net gain by No 50010 itself (and despite a lengthy stop at Reading), Paddington was reached 23min early. There was no wind assistance, the ETH was confirmed as being in use throughout, and the trailing load was re-checked twice on arrival. Between Cowley Bridge Junction and Whiteball the rhp was 2,285 over 18.65 miles at an average of 70.8mph. Accelerating from a permanent-way slack at Charlton Mackrell to Castle Cary, the locomotive produced 2,300rhp over 7 miles at 69.4mph, while the 10.5 miles from Edington to Patney were covered at an average 76mph, equating to an output of 2,320rhp. Note the consistency of these outputs. Allowing for ETH, the gross engine output was around 3,200bhp – nearly 20% higher than the nominal 2,700bhp rating. Three subsequent runs with the same locomotive within a year confirmed these figures.

Such a level of performance comes at a price, however, and the engine's main bearings expired after only 6,544 hours.

On 1 August 1985 No 50023 had charge of the 10.30 Penzance–Liverpool Lime Street – an 11-coach train that day. Climbing Whiteball it developed 2,350rhp, while accelerating to Bridgwater produced 2,175rhp. Top speed was 101mph at Yatton. With the same train on 26 August 1986, No 50005 had an extra coach and also developed 2,350rhp climbing Whiteball. Acceleration to Bridgwater saw 2,380rhp and superior running to that of No 50023. The speed reached 100mph before Uphill Junction (where No 50023 was only up to 95) before power was shut off for a conflicting movement at Worle Junction. No 50005 continued to Birmingham in similar lively fashion, topping the Lickey Incline at a remarkable 38mph.

Running between Bristol and Birmingham has not featured thus far, although the 1980s saw Class 50s in charge of most of the trains that changed traction at the latter location. It was a route not suited to showing off the class at its best, because speed was dropping against the grade on all the principal climbs, and it was clear that minimum speeds were no better (and possibly worse) than those achieved by other ETH Type 4s. Instead of copious personal recordings, a couple of trips from a broad selection timed by Keith Foster will illustrate train running. Mr Foster is a highly experienced and meticulous exponent of train-timing, and his records can thus be regarded as completely reliable.

On 7 December 1985 a shortage of Class 47s brought recently ex-works No 50031 on the 06.03 Paddington–Liverpool and 13.52 return to Portsmouth Harbour; this presented the opportunity to combine an outstanding performance with an unusual working, Mr Foster logging the return leg as far as Birmingham New Street. Principal interest centred on the section from Crewe to Whitmore Summit, and fortunately the train was put on the fast line. The passing time at Whitmore was 9min 34sec at 90mph. Clearly, thereafter the driver was not concentrating, because speed continued to rise to 105mph by Standon Bridge, where there was a slight easing to around 102.

Being just out of 'shop', No 50031 could be expected to be in fine fettle, and this was indeed the case. Power during the Whitmore climb was 2,130rhp, so, with ETH load added, engine output was around 2,850bhp. Whilst not as spectacular as that encountered on the journeys described previously, this was still abnormally high. The incidence of such high outputs was raised by the author with Doncaster staff, and an assurance given that there had been no change in the way engines were set up on the load bank.

The 07.20 Glasgow–Bristol Temple Meads offered a useful round trip from Birmingham with a Class 50, which took the return 15.48 service. On 12 July 1986 No 50009 had the usual 12-coach rake. Having left Gloucester on time, at Gloucester Yard Junction No 50009 suffered a 2½min delay occasioned by a

Van trains, conveying newspaper or parcels traffic, saw Class 50 power both day and night. At Exeter St Davids on 6 August 1985 No 50045 *Achilles* has charge of the 20.05 parcels from Bedwyn. Alongside is No 50010 *Monarch* with the 21.56 to Newton Abbot. *David N. Clough*

late-running Manchester–Paignton HST. The customary high speed with a '50' followed a strong acceleration up the grade past Standish Junction, Coaley being passed at 98mph; the rate then gradually fell away on the next uphill section to Rangeworthy, passed at 84, yet the lost time had nevertheless been recovered by Yate. Between Tuffley Junction site and Standish Junction, 2,450rhp was developed at 70.3mph. From MP113 to MP118 speed fell from 90.45mph to 85.5 against the grade, representing 2,150rhp; clearly No 50009 was performing as predicted in terms of giving maximum effort only during acceleration. Allowing for ETH, the locomotive would have been producing around 3,280bhp.

In the reverse direction, nearly a minute was gained between Temple Meads and Parkway, and a further 1½min to Cheltenham. Delays spoiled the next leg, but interest naturally focuses on the climb of Lickey. Accelerating from a check at Dunhampstead, No 50009 passed Stoke Works Junction at 71mph, the speed falling thereafter to 28 at Blackwell. This gave an average of 54.6mph but only 1,910rhp. In the northbound direction

there are really no stretches of sufficient length under full-power acceleration to offer a reliable calculation, but No 50009 was clearly master of its job by a considerable margin. (It must, however, be admitted that the minima at Rangeworthy (southbound) and Blackwell have been seen with Classes 45 and 47.)

Given one's absolute confidence in the accuracy of the train-timing data, just what was going on remained a mystery. As well as approaching Doncaster direct, the author had drawn the WR's attention to the over-powering of some locomotives, and the Region itself duly took this up with Doncaster, prompting a review of procedures. Thereafter, during setting-up in the test house, staff were told to make sure generator current was not showing as too high, even though the control resistance values were set correctly, and this seemed to solve the matter.

Counterbalancing demonstrations of abnormally high power, a series of journeys timed by Martin Beckett, mainly on the Waterloo line, will serve to show how inconsistent Class 50 performance could be. Mr Beckett commuted daily from Basingstoke and became an expert in

In 1986 No 50022 *Anson* passes through Colthorpe, near Newbury, with empty newspaper vans from the West Country bound for Old Oak Common.
D. E. Canning

timing trains along the entire route to Exeter. The recordings (shown right) were made during the period 1989-91.

The table represents the distillation of 152 estimates of power for all the class still engaged on passenger work at the time. The analysis reveals several anomalies. Power estimates between Westbourne Park and Southall on the WR are consistently lower than those for the same locomotive on the SR, and this confirms a personal view about the former section. Acceleration from low speed at Woking Junction to MP31 produced lower outputs than at a higher speed. There was marked inconsistency between different runs made over a short period with the same locomotive, and during the summer this cannot be explained by ETH demands. For tabulation here, a mean output has been taken across several runs with one machine. As expected, climbing Honiton Bank, with speed falling, produced lower power than on sections where the locomotive was accelerating.

How things had changed since the late 1970s, when many Class 50s were clearly under-performing. From the above sample, 50% were producing a 'normal' 2,650-2,750bhp, with the rest split between below (18.75%) and above (31.25%) the norm. Taking No 50001 by way of example, the table (right) takes seven performances during the summer of 1989 to show the degree of variation.

Mention of Porton Bank recalls the very high speeds run by a few drivers after track improvements in the mid-1980s. Although speed was officially limited to 90mph, the alignment and ride quality meant that 100mph was common, and reports circulated of occasions when locomotives were taken beyond the 120mph maximum that could be recorded on a Class 50 speedometer. Old Oak Common drivers were more disciplined, and speeds above prescribed maxima were very unusual. Schedules were undemanding of a Class 50, and running with the typical nine- and 10-car formations brought little that had not been seen during the 1970s.

Following their introduction, HSTs monopolised the centre platforms at Paddington; this gave a faster departure, because there was no need to snake over several crossovers to reach the down fast line. Unusually, on 4 September 1989, the

Class 50 power-output survey 1989-91							
Bhp	2,500	<2,600	Normal	>2,800	>2,900	>3,000	>3,100
Nº of instances	2	4	16	3	3	3	1

Gross engine output (bhp) for No 50001 during the summer of 1989							
Location	27/6	1/8	6/8	8/8	12/8	4/9	5/9	Average
Woking	2,730		2,840			2,840	2,870	2,820
Porton		3,040		2,960	2,870			2,960

Note:
'Woking' means Woking Junction to MP31
'Porton' means Salisbury Tunnel Junction to MP76

17.45 to Westbury had the luxury of leaving from Platform 5, which afforded a direct route onto the fast line. No 50033 had only eight vehicles – two fewer than the usual formation for this popular train. Royal Oak was passed in under a minute, and the 90mph mark attained by Southall. Although No 50033 was a bit below par, at about 2,550bhp, there was no difficulty in touching 101mph after Langley; thereafter a noticeable throttling-back prevented further acceleration, and after Burnham the Class 47-powered 17.42 Bristol had been caught up. Sensible driving now saw speed held at around 95mph to avoid further checks. The preceding service did not call at Reading and No 50033's driver was able to make an unhindered approach. Overall, the time was 26min 12sec and might have been under 26min, had the slower Class 47 not got in the way.

Signal over-running in 1983 whilst working short newspaper trains resulted in the class's being restricted to 95mph for a year. The only modifications made were cab stencilling and instrumentation markings to advise drivers of the lower limit, as seen on the cabside of No 50047 *Swiftsure*.
David N. Clough

CHANGING TIMES

With only a single platform and no loop until the autumn of 1986, Tisbury was one of the most remote locations on the Waterloo line. Needless to say, if a '50' failed *en route*, the most common place for this to happen was…Tisbury! In an attempt to minimise such occurrences, the SR duly banned historically unreliable locomotives from working the Waterloo services.

Memorably, on 18 July 1986 two Class 50s returned to their old haunts in the North West. No 50040 was on the 10.30 Penzance–Liverpool and had to work throughout due to the non-availability of the booked replacement Class 47 at Birmingham; it returned home on the 21.35FO to Penzance. Meanwhile No 50007 had been requested to appear at Carlisle Upperby's open day on the 19th. The 21.45 Bristol Temple Meads–Glasgow Central was used as far as Carlisle to move the machine (making it the first Class 50 working over Shap since No 50011's railtour appearance on 31 October 1981), which returned home on the 23.50 Glasgow Central–Bristol Temple Meads.

On 22 October 1986, due to the failure at Hereford of the Class 56 on the Pengam–Glasgow 'liner', Nos 50016 and 50041 were borrowed to work forward to Crewe, before returning on the balancing service; having thus missed their booked duty from Hereford, the '50s' eventually returned light to Old Oak Common.

In August 1986 No 50026 was selected to undergo the prototype 'F' exam at Laira, although it did not receive overhauled bogies or power unit. In October 1986 No 50034 became the second candidate and did receive an overhauled power unit. To facilitate power-unit lifts inside the depot, a 35-tonne crane was installed. Power units were transported to/from Doncaster Works by road.

The year 1987 proved to be an eventful one. From 1 January all BR traction was assigned to one of the newly created Sectors, and it soon emerged that the InterCity Sector did not want any Class 50s, preferring Class 47s instead. This left Class 50 allocations split between NSE (29), Provincial (6), Parcels (9), Departmental (2) and Railfreight (2). The figures in brackets note the Sector ownership by October, after a settling-down of reassignment of ownership and after two locomotives had been withdrawn, of which more anon. From the Summer timetable the class came off all InterCity diagrams, except for a few Saturday workings; in their place came extra Provincial Sector diagrams in the West of England and turns including Portsmouth Harbour–Waterloo – hardly exciting stuff for a class that had spent all its life on top-flight long-haul passenger services, and arguably a first nail in the coffin.

Classified overhauls at Doncaster came to an end with No 50048 on 18 March, although Nos 50019/37/44 subsequently

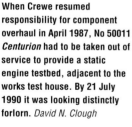

When Crewe resumed responsibility for component overhaul in April 1987, No 50011 *Centurion* had to be taken out of service to provide a static engine testbed, adjacent to the works test house. By 21 July 1990 it was looking distinctly forlorn. *David N. Clough*

visited the works for unclassified repairs or rectification. Crewe Works took over responsibility for Class 50 component overhauls, and No 50011 was sent there to act as a testbed for overhauled power units. It was due an 'F' exam, having run 393,325 miles and accumulated 8,827 TOPS hours since its general overhaul in April 1983. After a last working on 12 February, it spent several days on empty-stock movements at Paddington, before Laira carried out some maintenance. The locomotive then worked a parcels to Crewe and withdrawal – less than four years' service since refurbishment (far less than anyone had envisaged) and the first Class 50 to succumb. Some regret was expressed by the ship's company of HMS *Centurion*, who had presented replica badges for No 50011 as recently as May 1986, so, to resolve the matter, No 50040 *Leviathan* was renamed *Centurion* in July 1987.

By mid-1987 class availability was so poor that the BRB Director of Mechanical & Electrical Engineering took an interest. A crisis meeting was held in early June at which a number of proposals were tabled to deal with technical issues. The meeting also considered taking four locomotives out of traffic to allow cannibalisation and thus relieve a chronic shortage of spares. No 50020 had been stopped at Laira for four months awaiting materials and was

returned to traffic only by cannibalising No 50006. The latter suffered a main-generator failure on 4 June and became the second withdrawal, because, like Nos 50011 and 50014, it had not received repairs to its underframe fractures. BR's traction plan at the time envisaged the class's survival until 1992, with a phased run-down from 1987.

Sunday diversions sometimes saw Waterloo–Exeter-line trains routed via Southampton. On 17 February 1988 No 50020 *Revenge* heads away from Southampton with the 11.05 Plymouth–Brighton.
John Chalcraft

RAILFREIGHT EXPERIMENT

After a lengthy gestation period, the conversion of a locomotive for dedicated Railfreight use finally happened. Months had passed from initial confirmation of the proposal in 1986, and it had taken until February 1987 for Railfreight to sanction the experiment. It was to be done on the cheap, in that sanding gear – *de rigeur* for all new freight designs since 1970 – was not to be fitted. The only differences from a standard '50' were to be the fitting of Class 37/7 bogies, which had lower gearing and an 80mph top speed, and the derating of the engine to 2,400bhp. Just why some clever person at the Railway Technical Centre deemed this essential, to prevent exceeding the traction-motors' continuous-current limits, could not be fathomed by any engineer on the WR. Livery was to be Railfreight's new triple-grey livery in 'General' form. Nameplates would be yellow. Finally, the locomotive was to be renumbered into the 501xx series, to differentiate it from standard machines and avoid misallocation on inappropriate duties.

The selected locomotive was to undergo an 'F' exam, and Railfreight wanted to carry out trials in September. No 50050 was a candidate by virtue of having an 'F' exam during the summer but, being the former D400, was ruled out through sentiment. This put Nos 50043 and 50049 in the frame. The former needed an overhauled power unit, whereas the latter had received one during a visit to Doncaster in 1985. Crewe Works was proving slow in overhauling engines, so No 50049 was selected for conversion during August. If successful, this was to be replicated by other conversions. A range of possible duties was considered, notably stone bound for the SR from Meldon and Merehead quarries, as well as 'liner' trains and cement traffic. Replacement of pairs of Class 33s seems to have been an aim.

No 50149 seemed jinxed, suffering a minor main-generator flashover and also derailing during its first trial. Then the engine suffered a major failure. Desperate to keep to the launch date of 15 October, the WR had No 50014 sidelined and its power unit, suitably derated, fitted into 50149. Already earmarked for withdrawal, No 50014 had nevertheless been very reliable just prior to its demise, running 13,789 miles and accumulating 289 TOPS hours during August – remarkable figures for a locomotive not engaged on long-distance InterCity services.

On 18 October No 50149 was put through its paces on Warminster Bank, between Westbury and Salisbury; the WR gradient profile gave 1 in 70 as the ruling gradient, but the SR quoted 1 in 66. A maximum load of 1,275 tonnes was taken, with three restarts attempted on each of three trips. The day was showery, and the locomotive suffered a number of traction-motor overloads and engine shutdowns, together with severe wheelslip, particularly where oil had contaminated the railhead. The driver avoided excessive current, and just why the lower-geared traction motors should have overloaded was not clear. Some restarts were successful, but during others wheelslip was so severe as to cause sparking at the railhead. Of course, refurbishment had robbed the locomotive of systems that would have helped, notably the tractive-effort control and low-speed wheelslip correction; when the rails were sanded

manually, No 50149 made clean starts. Needless to say, the experiment was not replicated – one 117-tonne Class 50 Co-Co could not provide the same adhesion as two 75-tonne Bo-Bos and hence haul the same weight of train. The cost of refitting sanding gear was estimated at £14,000, but Railfreight deemed this too much; had it decided otherwise, then the last years of Class 50 would have been quite different. No 50149 subsequently deputised for collision-damaged Class 37s on Cornish china-clay traffic until being converted back to a standard Class 50 in February 1989.

RUN-DOWN GATHERS PACE

Perhaps surprisingly, No 50046 re-emerged from its 'F' exam still in Laira's version of 'large logo' blue, with black roof and red buffer beams. It was said that this was because it was a standby for Royal Train duty, although the class had never had the honour of hauling a train with Royalty aboard until No 50007 did so on 5 May 1988. The 1987/8 financial year was the last in which such major work was carried out, and thereafter an 'E' exam was the most extensive attention undertaken. No 50003 received the last 'F' exam and was released on 8 March 1988.

Unique Class 50/1 No 50149 spent most of 1988 working freights in Cornwall, with some diagrams taking it as far afield as Gloucester. It is seen on 4 May bringing a china-clay train off the branch at Burngullow Junction. *M. J. Beckett*

The cessation of major overhauls was matched by a refusal to spend large sums on repairing collision and derailment damage. By 1988 any mishap that would previously have seen a locomotive 'shopped' brought concern of impending withdrawal. No 50012, for example, fell into the Old Oak Common turntable, but the damage was patched up.

From the Summer 1988 timetable the Provincial Sector withdrew from sponsorship of Class 50. This eliminated diagrams around Bristol and the West Country on Class 2 trains. At the same time InterCity cut back further its use of the class. When the contract for railborne transportation of newspapers ended in July 1988, this eliminated more Class 50 diagrams on trains that started at Paddington and Waterloo. The Parcels Sector thus had a reduced need for the class, and NSE added Waterloo–Salisbury to its utilisation.

At a meeting to discuss the NSE traction situation in April 1988 it was observed that Class 50 was the hardest-worked locomotive fleet on BR, averaging 2,000 TOPS hours and 94,000 miles annually, with a failure rate of around 9,000mpc. At the time, the Laira locomotives had the edge on those at Old Oak Common in terms of reliability. By contrast, NSE's Class 47s were achieving just 1,500 TOPS hours and 75,000 miles annually, at a rate of 9,000mpc; the view was that these would be even less satisfactory on the Waterloo line than were the Class 50s, and for this reason the latter were to be retained until 1992, when new DMUs were expected to arrive.

The chronic shortage of spare power units continued to cripple availability, part of the problem being the very long lead times for EE to supply components. For whatever reason, a number of engines suffered severe failure, with a connecting rod coming through the side of the block, and were thus written off. The unit from DP2, IH5567, met its fate in this way whilst in No 50037. Major engine and main-generator failures came far faster than anticipated. This caused a hiatus, because Crewe Works had an agreed programme with NSE for these components, yet this was proving to be a serious underestimate of demand.

Despite the difficulties, a national shortage of diesel locomotives had the effect of postponing further withdrawals aimed at reducing Class 50 numbers to the National Traction Plan target of 38. For the first time a dedicated pool was selected for Waterloo-line diagrams in an attempt to improve reliability; of these, all bar No 50019 were Laira-allocated locomotives that had recently received an overhaul or 'F' exam.

Notwithstanding the doubts expressed at the April meeting, continuing availability

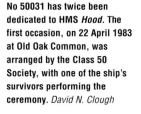

No 50031 has twice been dedicated to HMS *Hood*. The first occasion, on 22 April 1983 at Old Oak Common, was arranged by the Class 50 Society, with one of the ship's survivors performing the ceremony. *David N. Clough*

problems meant that Laira duly received three Class 47/4s for a comparative trial on Waterloo services. Inevitably, the first few months brought many failures with the Brush machines, and some Exeter drivers demanded a '50' instead. The interlopers' lower fuel capacity meant they often had to take fuel mid-diagram, while brake blocks had to be changed every other day, so the '50s' continued on borrowed time until ScotRail could release its Class 47/7s, which had larger fuel tanks.

A tightening of diagramming by the WR power controllers was implemented from January 1989. This meant that the 16 examples allocated to Old Oak Common were largely confined to services out of Paddington, whilst NSE's 13 Laira-based locomotives covered the Waterloo line. Meanwhile the Civil Engineer imposed a 60mph limit on his fleet of Class 50s and so reduced their usefulness for passenger turns. One effect of Sector-pool allocation

was that there was no respite for those locomotives on the Waterloo line. Previously, the policy had been to rotate the time spent on such turns, because of their arduous nature. Between Waterloo and Basingstoke the track was rough due to heavy use by EMUs, and this caused a large diesel to bounce – far from ideal for good performance by the electrical machinery. West of Salisbury there were 13 stations at an average distance of seven miles apart, which meant running at full power for short intervals before heavy braking – again, a lethal combination for a large diesel engine and a highly stressed main generator. Finally, Southern drivers were, reportedly, accustomed to using just two power-controller positions – 'off' and 'full'. This driving technique was not that recommended by EE and also not ideal for the engine and main generator.

By 1989 the steps taken in 1988 by Mike Winstock, NSE's Class 50 engineer, to

Tied in with the Haymarket depot open day, Pathfinder's 'Scots Streaker II' charter ran from Plymouth to Edinburgh via the East Coast on 25 August 1985. No 50030 *Repulse* enters Waverley station at journey's end. *C. R. Holland*

Above: **When No 50033 was repainted from large logo livery to NSE style at the start of 1990, Old Oak Common left the nameplate in its original position. This gave the impression that the name** *Glorious* **applied to NSE, as can just be discerned in this picture. The locomotive is seen passing Winchfield on 7 September 1990 with the 13.18 Salisbury–Waterloo.** *David N. Clough*

Right: **A shortage of WR Class 47/4s during early 1988 brought a Class 50 to Manchester Piccadilly on the 07.03 from Paddington. On 9 March No 50044** *Exeter* **prepares to back onto its return working, the 14.01 to Stafford.** *David N. Clough*

improve reliability were beginning to bear fruit, with a 9,000mpc rate being sustained. After their settling-in period, however, the three Class 47s were 33% better, at 12,000mpc. The latter type also needed less attention to remedy defects, whilst the '50s' often needed major surgery, such as traction-motor or main-generator exchanges. Nevertheless, a '50' could, theoretically, take up power from rest some 16sec quicker than could a '47', which mounted up when there were 16 intermediate stations.

On a like-for-like basis Class 47 was cheaper to run than Class 50, and NSE was keen to put the most favourable business case for acquiring new DMU stock for the route; it therefore suited NSE to retain Class 50 on the Waterloo line to demonstrate better savings by substituting DMUs. Of course, a further factor was that other Sectors were unable to cascade ETH Class 47s in sufficient numbers during 1989. Other factors also came into play: Laira was experienced with Class 50 but less so with Class 47 and knew that cascaded Brush Type 4s would need overhauls. History records that, when Class 47/7s (many given 'F' exams) did take over, their reliability and availability were no better than those of the Class 50s.

May 1989 brought more Sector-pool changes, Mr Winstock picking his first team for the Waterloo line. All Waterloo–Salisbury trains fell to Class 50s, and the overall Waterloo-line requirement became 20. Old Oak Common gave up locomotives to augment the Laira fleet, as well as providing two for the Departmental Sector in exchange for the latter's relinquishing two machines for the Waterloo pool. NSE now had No 50007, and it was not long before Sector Director Chris Green spotted its non-corporate colours at Waterloo. At a meeting at Laira in June, he said he wanted it repainted to standard NSE colours. Area Fleet Manager Geoff Hudson was at pains to point out that it was the depot's flagship and that morale would be affected by its loss. As a compromise, Mr Green suggested repainting in corporate NSE colours but also renaming as *Pride of Laira*. However, as an HST power car was due to be bestowed thus, Mr Green eventually acquiesced, provided No 50007's paintwork was kept immaculate.

In mid-1989 the problems encountered with the new Class 155 DMUs brought Class 50s back onto Provincial Sector services in the West of England for a time. Twelve months on, however, more of Old

After Network SouthEast dispensed with the services of No 50019 *Ramillies*, on 22 February 1989, the Departmental Sector paid for Laira to repaint it, in view of its shabby state. The depot produced a new livery variation, dubbed 'Laira blue', featuring a white roof, which soon became black with exhaust particles. This picture, taken near Okehampton on 5 April 1990, illustrates the result. *C. M. Parsons, Dave Mitchell collection*

Oak Common's fleet could be released from Thames-line activity, because more Class 47s had arrived from other Sectors. Nos 50023/35 were the last to be allocated and moved to Laira on 12 July 1990. The latter survived until 3 August, after 22 years in traffic, and had covered the remarkable total of 404,492 miles – 10% more than other Class 50s – since its last works overhaul in July 1986. Although precise figures are not available, this locomotive must have exceeded 2 million miles from new.

The Departmental Sector's plans to replace its '50s' with Class 37s took a step forward on 15 October, when Nos 50023/32/42 were withdrawn. The last had received an overhauled power unit only a couple of months beforehand. NSE took No 50023's engine to replace a defective one in No 50037 and on 21 September withdrew its own No 50045 to provide a power unit for No 50003.

BIG CUTBACKS IN 1991
At the start of 1991 the Departmental Sector retained Nos 50008/15/31/6/46, whilst NSE had 19 still on its books, so just under half the class remained in traffic. On 25 January Departmental gave up its survivors to NSE, though Nos 50008/15 were retained solely for charter use for a year and had received repaints earlier in the month. Old Oak Common continued to service locomotives that ended their day at Waterloo, and on 23 March Nos 50001/33/48 were there for attention. The decision to fit overhauled power units to Nos 50033 and 50046 was perhaps surprising. The former's engine then gave much trouble and required a visit by works staff to carry out rectification work – shades of the old days!

Sidelined for months following a main-generator failure, No 50050 finally returned to traffic on 6 April, RAIL magazine having sponsored a repaint into original blue livery, complete with D400 numbers. Laira had not finished with repaints, because No 50031 was spruced up the following month to commemorate the 50th anniversary of the sinking of HMS *Hood*. Faults saw Nos 50003/7/27 sidelined in early July, and on the 21st five more diagrams went over to ETH Class 47s; this day was possibly the first since 1974 that

No 50008 *Thunderer* heads up the former Southern main line at Crediton with a ballast train from Meldon Quarry to Exeter Riverside Yard on 26 November 1990. *Dave Mitchell*

Laira did not turn out a Class 50 for service. Behind the July cutbacks was a cost-cutting drive within NSE, and the lower running-costs of the Class 47s now mattered most. Old Oak Common had received a rag-bag of high-hours Class 47/4s, mainly from Railfreight. As soon as one of these was accepted by the Depot Engineer for reliable service, it would replace a Thames-line Class 47/7, which, in turn, would migrate to the Waterloo line and displace a Class 50. Thus NSE was able to discard a large batch of '50s' in one short spell during July and August. Aside from the July failures already mentioned, locomotives due a major exam (such as No 50049) came out of traffic.

By late September No 50033 was in need of traction-motor repairs, No 50050 was again stopped after another major main-generator flashover, and Nos 50029/30/46 were available, with two usually in traffic. At the Laira open day Peter Field, head of NSE South West, and Geoff Hudson discussed the popularity of the class with enthusiasts and the potential for generating revenue, the re-launch of D400 earlier in the year having caused a

significant increase in ticket sales. Out of this meeting came the idea to retain several examples for charter use. Mr Field sanctioned No 50050's return to traffic and a 'look at' the feasibility of doing likewise with No 50007.

In the latter part of 1991 Nos 50008/15 made occasional trips on Engineer's trains, Sandite workings and the occasional passenger substitution. More than a wry smile passed across the lips of Class 50 fans when 1992 arrived and NSE was forced to retain the three surviving serviceable '50s' (Nos 50030/3/50) because of appalling Class 47/7 availability. The Waterloo line was proving every bit as taxing for the new order as it had for the old. Almost unheard of was two locomotives being in works for main-generator repairs, because the Brush generator was generally most reliable. Highly regrettable was a senior NSE manager's assertion during a BBC Radio 4 interview that the dreadful service quality at the time was due to Class 50 performance; none was working! When the author challenged this publicly there was a hasty retraction, but Old Oak Common was annoyed that the high failure

No 50041 *Bulwark* will always be remembered as the locomotive involved in the Paddington derailment of 22 November 1983. This picture shows the scene the following day. *David N. Clough collection*

Having suffered a main-generator failure in 1990, No 50007 *Sir Edward Elgar* was repaired by NSE only on the basis that it should be a project for Laira's 18 apprentices. Its bogies were exchanged with those from No 50046 *Ajax*, as seen here. *Paul Furtek*

rate of its fleet had been exposed. Whereas Laira allocated one riding fitter to each shift during the day, Old Oak Common was providing twice as many, supplemented by those from Laira, to keep the Class 47s running. Despite this fact, clearly it was fair game officially to say that Class 50 was unreliable and the cause of all the Waterloo line's problems, but the same was not allowed for Class 47.

On 2 January 1992 No 50029 suffered a major engine failure, whilst No 50046 had earlier been taken out of service to provide a replacement main generator in order to resuscitate No 50007. The former had been a popular engine with enthusiasts, the latter much less so since its renaming in 1984. Hence the decision to sideline No 50046 was not well received. The work on No 50007 was set up as a project for Laira's 18 apprentices, suitably supervised. When the replacement power unit was started for the first time, a bolt that had been left by accident in a main-generator brushbox scored a 3/16in groove in the armature. Fortunately the armature had been built oversize by Crewe, allowing it to be ground down to remove the groove; this was the first such grinding *in situ* on depot and proved successful. On 12 March No 50007 made a trial run from Laira to Newton Abbot in grey primer and was nearly ready to return to traffic. By now only No 50050 was in traffic, but not very often.

As had been laid down five years previously in the National Traction Plan, NSE withdrew its support for service use at the end of March, but a finale weekend was arranged for 23/24 May. Postponement until then was to permit this to take place on the middle day of a Bank Holiday weekend, the objective being to avoid disruption to other passengers by the presence of hordes of enthusiasts. On the 21st, however, No 50007 was turned out to rescue the 09.15 Glasgow Central–Plymouth HST, which had failed near Totnes. On the 24th Nos 50007/50 took the last working, the 16.55 ex Waterloo, forward from Salisbury to Exeter, and so the curtain came down on timetabled Class 50 use in BR ownership. Who could have guessed what was to come?

THE RAILTOUR YEARS

With the support of Geoff Hudson and agreement from Peter Field of NSE, it was agreed that Nos 50007/33/50 could be retained for railtours. This brought some interesting trips and varied guises. Laira had to maintain the records for the trio, keeping careful tabs on mileage. Part of the arrangement was that no cost would fall to NSE, meaning that charter revenue had to cover all Laira's costs. Mr Hudson budgeted on 12 charters per year, which would finance an annual 'B' exam for each locomotive, plus an 'A' exam before each journey. Tests by Laira had shown main-

Above: **No 50007 made a light-engine run in primer after mechanical work had been completed, being seen here at Totnes.** *Paul Furtek*

Left: **The finished product. No 50007 at the NRM during the summer of 1993.** *Geoff Hudson*

Above: **Pathfinder's two 'Fellsman' railtours brought the class back to old LMR haunts. On 23 April 1988 Nos 50024 *Vanguard* and 50050 *Fearless* cross Ribblehead Viaduct on their way home from Carlisle.** *David N. Clough*

Right: **Before Nos 50015 and 50008 could be used for railtours during 1991, Geoff Hudson insisted they be repainted. No 50008 received Laira-style blue, whilst No 50015 acquired full Departmental colours. The pair are seen near Abergavenny with the 'Hoover Hoop' tour in October 1991.** *David N. Clough*

generator volts rose sharply above 80mph, so, to minimise the risk of a flashover, the little fleet was limited to 75mph. In addition, the engines were derated by reducing maximum revs by 50 to 800rpm.

Although most of the charters ran successfully, the 'Court Chester' on 13 June 1992 ended in a shambles. For various reasons the train got seriously behind schedule and arrived at Bedford at 23.45. Its route towards Oxford was now closed, and station staff curtailed the train. Strong protests ensued, causing the staff to summon the police. This backfired on them, however, because the police sided with the passengers and directed that the train continue to St Pancras.

For several reasons it was decided that the end of the 1993/4 financial year was to be the finale for the remaining Class 50s. One of the final tours was over old haunts from Birmingham to Glasgow, and a nice touch was the repainting of Nos 50033 and 50050 into original-style Rail blue. To keep Laira's costs within budget, Locomaster Profiles agreed to sponsor the work on No 50033, whilst Pathfinder Tours contributed towards No 50050.

During the summer of 1993 No 50007 had been put on display at the National Railway Museum, becoming the first BR locomotive to be exhibited thus while still in traffic. The NRM subsequently expressed a desire to have a Class 50 as a permanent exhibit but requested a locomotive in NSE livery. This singled out No 50033, which carried these colours at the time, but later the NRM decided it wanted its exhibit in 'large logo' style. No 50033 was thus prepared at Laira for this role, and a first-class restoration carried out, while No 50050 was also returned to this guise. On 19 March 1994 the duo worked to York, and the day after No 50033 took a charter to Scarborough and back before entering the museum. On its way home No 50050 was called upon to rescue a failed InterCity Class 47/8 at Ashchurch – much to the chagrin of Bath Road's Area Fleet Manager, John Cronin, who had previously been Geoff Hudson's boss!

The curtain finally came down on 26 March 1994, when Nos 50007 and 50050 worked a Charter from Waterloo to Penzance and back to Paddington, arriving just before midnight. Drivers clamoured to be part of the wake, and all went well. Coincidentally, InterCity staged a special event at Paddington earlier in the day to mark its own demise in the lead-up to privatisation, but Chris Green, by then InterCity Director, admitted privately that he would probably have preferred to be at Waterloo instead! Such was the feeling of professional railwaymen for the Class 50.

Ready for the NRM. No 50033 *Glorious* posed with the staff at Laira in March 1994.
Paul Furtek

Right: **What was thought at the time to be the main-line finale. On 26 March 1994 Nos 50050 *Fearless* and 50007 *Sir Edward Elgar* power through Tisbury with Pathfinder Tours' 08.52 Waterloo–Penzance '50 Terminator'.** *G. F. Gillham*

Below: **Laira sometimes repainted locomotives into its own variation of 'large logo' livery, featuring black roof and red buffer-beams. No 50008 *Thunderer* had just been given this treatment when caught departing Newton Abbot for Laira carriage sidings after working the Paddington–Paignton 'Torbay Express' in September 1986.** *David N. Clough*

Above: When Chris Green moved from ScotRail to the London & South East Sector he rebranded the latter as Network SouthEast, with a livery of red, white and blue, which over the years would see three variants. In original NSE guise (and with unique blue nameplate), No 50032 *Courageous* passes Twyford with the 17.20 Paddington–Banbury on 15 May 1990. *David N. Clough*

Left: The second variant of NSE livery appeared in 1987 and dispensed with the swept-up bands at the cab ends, as seen here on No 50030 *Repulse*, passing Vauxhall with the 09.15 Waterloo–Exeter St Davids in January 1988. Westminster Abbey and Big Ben are in the background. *David N. Clough*

Above: The original NSE light blue was found to fade very quickly, and from 1989 this was changed to a darker shade. No 50035 *Ark Royal* had recently been repainted when captured at around 100mph near Maidenhead on a freezing 6 April 1990. The train is the 17.45 Paddington–Westbury. *David N. Clough*

Right: No 50026 *Indomitable* works hard accelerating the 18.12 Paddington–Banbury through South Ruislip on 10 May 1990. *Chris Shaw*

Left: **Typical Waterloo-line scenery at Milborne Port. No 50028 *Tiger* heads the 09.15 Waterloo–Exeter St Davids on 8 September 1990.**
David N. Clough

Below: **Reduced InterCity demand from the summer of 1987 brought an increase in Class 50 appearances in South Wales. These were on Portsmouth–Cardiff trains that changed locomotives at Bristol Temple Meads and on vans from Milford Haven to Old Oak Common Carriage Sidings. However, another interesting duty at the time was the summer-dated 07.05 Carmarthen–Paddington service, on which No 50017 *Royal Oak* is seen passing Undy on 15 August 1987.**
David N. Clough

Right: **Both out-of-course and booked freight activity grew in the 1980s, notably after InterCity ceased using the class. On 3 September 1981 No 50036** *Victorious* **stands at Streatham Common with a Norwood–Acton freight.**
David N. Clough collection

Below: **No 50002** *Superb* **was recently ex works on 8 August 1985 when deputed to haul a Reading West–Acton Yard freight – a convenient way of returning it to Old Oak Common after it had worked the 11.15 Leeds–Portsmouth between Birmingham New Street and Reading. Such a diagram was quite common at the time.**
A. N. Middleton

Above: **Cornwall was the only place where the TPO could be photographed on the move. No 50008** *Thunderer* **departs Penzance with the 19.24 up service on 10 August 1984.** *Dave. Mitchell*

Left: **The TPO again, this time behind No 50049** *Defiance* **at Copperhouse on 14 August 1986.** *C. R. Holland*

Right: Nos 50042 *Triumph* and 50040 *Leviathan* at Scorrier on 14 August 1986 with the 12.10 Penzance–Glasgow parcels, which was diagrammed for a Class 50 in Cornwall.
C. R. Holland

Far right: Another quirky fill-in job was the Exeter Riverside–Dover china clay polybulks. On 17 September 1986 No 50017 *Royal Oak* approaches Heywood Road Junction, at the east end of the Westbury loop.
John Chalcraft

Below: The Departmental Sector had an allocation for engineers' traffic. Nos 50031 *Hood* and 50015 *Valiant* head the 14.37 Bristol East Depot–Exeter Riverside Yard at Brent on 21 August 1990. *C. R. Holland*

Far left: **Engineering work in Patchway Tunnels near Bristol was planned for two full weekends during August 1984 A single locomotive would have had insufficient fuel to run continuously for that time, so pairs of Class 50s were used on both occasions. Nos 50018** *Resolution* **and 50005** *Collingwood* **performed the first duty.** *C. R. Holland*

Left: **The Bristol West Depot–Swindon Freightliner was, for a time, a Class 50 turn. No 50044** *Exeter* **passes Pyle Hill, Bristol, on 20 August 1987.** *C. R. Holland*

Below: **In the late 1980s the class sometimes substituted for a DMU on the Barnstaple branch. On 19 July 1990 No 50042** *Triumph* **pauses at Lapford with the 14.14 Barnstaple–Exmouth.** *Richard Holmes*

Above: During the late 1980s the 07.12 Newton Abbot–Exeter St Davids was often booked for two locomotives, in order to get a second locomotive to Exeter for Waterloo-line duties. It also gave riding inspectors the opportunity to trial a machine after maintenance. The familiar Langstone Rock vantage-point was used here to record Nos 50016 *Barham* and 50029 *Renown* on 24 July 1989.
Richard Holmes

Right: Fancy a job? No 50050 *Fearless* under repair at Laira in March 1992.
Geoff Hudson collection

8 Private Ownership

During their time on the LMR the Class 50s were anything but popular with enthusiasts, who were conspicuous by their absence from the front coach of trains. Interest began to grow after naming in 1978/9. As always, this can take different forms with railways. One young woman used to 'feed' Smarties to her favourite, No 50035, by putting the sweets on the cab window frame!

Formation of the Class 50 Locomotive Group in 1981 focused interest, and membership grew quickly – to over 900 in a year. As one of the officers, the author realised that the Group had severe financial problems, and he was instrumental in winding up its affairs in late 1983, forming the Class 50 Society in January 1984 as its successor. Shortly afterwards the Class 50 Locomotive Association was formed, and these two organisations were the first to give thought to possible preservation. In 1989 they were joined by the Fifty Fund as class withdrawals gathered pace and a means of securing the future for one or more examples became a priority.

Early withdrawals were stripped by BR for useable components and were thus unfit for preservation. Clearance for sale to preservation groups came after BR was satisfied there was no asbestos risk. In the spring of 1990 Nos 50008/19/35 were offered for sale, based on known interest, but shortly afterwards No 50008 was taken off the list by BR for continued use. No 50019 was bought by the Class 50 Locomotive Association, and No 50035 by the Fifty Fund. No 50019 went to the Tunbridge Wells & Eridge Railway, whilst the Fund had set up a base at the former BR depot at St Leonards.

Prompted by the mass withdrawals in the summer of 1991, Geoff Hudson, aided by Mike Woodhouse, ensured that locomotives known to be of interest for preservation were not cannibalised at Laira. Soon afterwards, Nos 50002/27/31/42/9 were put out to tender. Although latterly a Departmental machine, No 50042 had received an overhauled power unit only a month or so before withdrawal. All the others offered for sale were also in full working order. No 50002 went to the Devon Diesel Society, based on the Torbay Steam Railway at Paignton. Mike Fuller acquired No 50027 and moved it to the Mid Hants Railway. Private buyers (who have requested anonymity) took over No 50031 but placed it in the care of the

No 50027 *Lion* at Alresford on the Mid Hants Railway on 17 May 1992 – its first day in traffic since purchase from BR.
M. J. Beckett

131

Fifty Fund at St Leonards. A group based on the Bodmin & Wenford Railway took No 50042. Finally, the Class 50 Society's bid for No 50049 was accepted. To formalise ownership, it was transferred immediately to a new company, Project Defiance Ltd, set up to reflect the shares bought by those who had contributed financially, with the Society remaining the largest shareholder. Restoration was undertaken at Laira.

The next tranche of Class 50s offered for sale were not generally in such good condition. Among them were Nos 50021/44, which had gone to Stratford depot for stripping but had hardly been touched. Whilst some went for scrap, others were saved. These were Nos 50017 (John Kennedy, Thingley Junction), 50021 (50021 Group, Mid Hants Railway), 50026 (Mike Fuller, Mid Hants Railway), 50043 (D318 Group, Tyseley) and 50044 (Fifty Fund, St Leonards). Subsequently Nos 50008 and 50015 became the property of Pete Waterman and the Manchester Class 50 Group respectively and went to the East Lancashire Railway.

In 1989 Robert Hurst had formed Operation Collingwood as an engineering-training base, using Class 50s to serve as the training equipment. The charity eventually managed to secure Nos 50029/30 from Laira in a competitive tender and Nos 50001/23/40/45 that Booth's had taken to Rotherham for scrap; none of these was in working order. No 50029's air-brake equipment had already been bought for use on LNER 'A3' steam locomotive No 4472 *Flying Scotsman*, and it also had a severely damaged engine. No 50030 had reputedly suffered main-generator damage, whilst the other four examples had been cannibalised extensively.

After the railtour era came to an end in March 1993 No 50007 was bought by the Class 40 Appeal and moved to Butterley on the Midland Railway Centre. An employee of Dutch Railways, Harry Schneider, secured No 50050 and considered initially taking it to the Netherlands for railtour use. By 1995, a total of 23 Class 50s – 46% – had moved into new ownership, including No 50033 at the NRM.

Preserving a machine as complex as a Class 50 was always bound to be a challenge. This was even more so for some of the new owners, who were ill resourced, in terms both of expertise and of spares. For a variety of reasons, changes took place in the ownership and location of many examples. D9000 Locomotives Ltd entered into an agreement with the Devon

Making a guest appearance on the Paignton & Dartmouth Railway, No 50042 *Triumph* departs Churston with a goods train on 16 October 1993.
G. F. Gillham

Left: **No 50031** *Hood* **at Cardiff Canton on 10 June 1998, just prior to making its first run for Valley Lines on the 17.05 Cardiff to Rhymney.** *A. N. Middleton*

Below: **Project Defiance had to remove the power unit from No 50149 to enable the defective main generator to be repaired. On 2 September 1994 the unit is lifted out at Williton on the West Somerset Railway. This operation led by Chris Holland PDL's Technical Director, won plaudits from WR depot staff because such work was regarded as a major task even for a fully equipped BR depot.** *David N. Clough*

No 50035 *Ark Royal* is the favourite machine of the highly respected chairman of the Fifty Fund, Jonathan Dunster, as well as of the author (who is Chairman of both the Class 50 Society and Project Defiance Ltd). It manages to clock up thousands of miles annually on the Severn Valley Railway.   *A. N. Middleton*

Diesel Society to return No 50002 to the main line; this never happened, and the locomotive lay idle at Barrow Hill museum, for many years. No 50008 moved initially to Longsight depot and then to Crewe South carriage sheds for main-line running. It was transferred to VSOE, but restoration has made very slow progress over nearly 10 years. Plans to ship it to a new home in Peru (as part of a local VSOE tie-up) have been abandoned, and the owners have offered it for sale or lease.

No 50017 was restored to working order by Project Defiance volunteers on the West Somerset Railway. Dr Kennedy then placed it with VSOE at Crewe for use on the latter's special trains, until VSOE reverted to the use of EWS traction. No 50017 has not run since then and is currently at Tyseley. Both Fragonset Railways and D9000 Locomotives Ltd have flirted with its use on the main line.

No 50019's owners decided to find pastures new at the Mid Norfolk Railway after resuscitating their acquisition. No 50021 moved from the Mid Hants Railway to the Gloucestershire & Warwickshire Railway, where it was restored to working order. It then went to the Bo'ness & Kinneil Railway, where a severe ETH-generator failure curtailed activity, and in 2002 it moved to Tyseley. Mike Fuller moved No 50027 to the

North Yorkshire Moors Railway and sold No 50026 to Paul Spracklen, who relocated the locomotive to the MoD base at Bicester. No 50043 was partly cannibalised as a means of raising money for the restoration of Class 40 No D318 and was then sold to Chris Long, who moved it to the Pontypool & Blaenavon Railway. With no restoration for several years, David Hurd bought it but soon sold it to Paul Spracklen for spares and eventual scrap. After a spell of main-line running on charters and spot-hire work under the auspices of D9000 Locomotives Ltd, No 50050 has been sidelined since 2000.

Operation Collingwood never managed to acquire the anticipated financial backing and became moribund. By August 2000 Robert Hurst was no longer involved, and the author was appointed a trustee, with a view to winding up the charity's affairs by an orderly disposal of its locomotives. Nos 50001/23/40/5 were sold back to Booth's, which then sold No 50023 (heavily stripped and with the severely damaged original DP2 engine) to Gareth Griffiths; it is kept at Barrow Hill museum for restoration. No 50040 passed through several further hands, including Cotswold Rail and David Hurd, and is now the property of a mystery owner, being based at Coventry Railway Museum. Paul Spracklen took over No 50045 for spares before it was finally cut up by Booth's, which also scrapped No 50001. In 2002 Operation Collingwood sold Nos 50029/30 to the Renown Repulse Restoration Group, and these are now undergoing restoration at Peak Rail.

The Fifty Fund moved No 50031 to the Severn Valley Railway, where it made its debut in May 1992. It was later joined by No 50044, the line becoming the Fund's new base. On 1 November 1997 No 50031 made its main-line debut on a Birmingham International–Plymouth charter, and June 1998 saw the locomotive go on hire to the Valley Lines in South Wales, where it was joined in 1999 by No 50044. Prior to this the latter had been restored to close to as-built external condition by the removal of the front-end jumper connections and return of the headcode box and bodyside sand fillers. It has since been blighted by two main-generator failures (whereby field coils have gone to earth due to the condition of the insulation), requiring removal of the power unit. Meanwhile the long-term restoration of No 50035 progressed and it too was moved to the Severn Valley Railway. Nos 50031/44 continue to be certified for main-line use and run between six and 12 charters annually as part of a carefully managed programme. They are passed to run at 90mph on the national network but are generally limited to 80mph by the Fund.

After return to Railfreight triple-grey livery and renumbering, No 50149 spent a spell at Allied Steel & Wire's Cardiff works before finding a home on the West Somerset Railway. Like No 50044, its main-generator field coils have twice gone to earth due to age, needing removal and specialist repair. In the mid-1980s Clive Burrows at Old Oak Common implemented a different method of aligning the brush gear with the main-generator armature, and he believed this helped reduce the risk of flashovers. This technique was adopted by Project Defiance and has since been extended to the Fifty Fund's fleet after Project Defiance joined forces with the Fund, although both organisations retain their independence. No 50149 travelled to the Severn Valley Railway for the Autumn 1999 Diesel Gala, and the SVR is currently its home (as it remains for Nos 50031/35/44). It made its main-line debut in September 2000 when paired with No 50031 as part of a charter from Birmingham to Glasgow for the Polmadie open day. Reminiscent of February 1994, the '50s' were repainted into all-over

No 50050 *Fearless* near Breydon Water, Norfolk, on 10 July 1999 whilst on hire to Anglia Railways. *J. Cordle*

A 1,300-tonne load and the banks between Bescot and Kidderminster to contend with? No problem – Nos 50049 and 50031 are in charge! The pair prepare to depart for the Severn Valley Railway with the auto-ballaster train. *A. N. Middleton*

blue livery and carried their original numbers at one end. Both locomotives spent some time at the depot, where No 50021 was also on show.

When the Severn Valley Railway required ballast in 2001 for permanent-way renewal, the train was brought from Bescot Yard onto the railway by Nos 50031 and 50049. The operation was repeated on 2 September 2003 and the load (including 'dead' Class 52 No 1015, returning to Kidderminster after exhibition) was c1,300 tons, handled with ease over the 1-in-70 grades of the Cradley Heath route.

By the end of 2002 accumulated mileages for Nos 50031/5/44/9 were as follows:

Year	50031	50035	50044	50049
1992	352			
1993	716			
1994	505		476	188
1995	1,202		94	433
1996	458	63	557	339
1997	792		781	
1998	9,092		839	
1999	3,576		3,089	541
2000	1,801			1,588
2001	4,286	1,041		3,426
2002	7,363	1,810		6,374
Total	30,143	2,914	5,836	12,889

Source: Jonathan Dunster and Richard Holmes

Currently 20 representatives survive. In the author's view, this is too many for the available resources, notably key spares. Whilst some are clearly very long-term restoration projects, the viability of a few of these must be in doubt. Even VSOE found that keeping a Class 50 in traffic (and in a reliable condition) was not easy. So long as their owners can provide manpower and money, Nos 50007/15/9/27/42 should manage to potter along on a preserved railway; all appear to be in working order. Paul Spracklen is making strides towards a full overhaul of No 50026, and this will undoubtedly run again, possibly even on the main line.

Without question, the alliance between the Fifty Fund and Project Defiance provides the best bet for securing the future for Nos 50031/5/44/9, both on the main line and on a preserved railway. VSOE certainly has the capability to resurrect No 50008, but with what end in view? Although Dr Kennedy is said to want No 50017 to return to the national network, he currently lacks the backing of a proper management team. The NRM wishes to divest itself of No 50033 as surplus to requirements. As for the rest, their prospects can perhaps best be described as 'outlook uncertain'.

Above: On 16 August 2003 Nos 50049 and 50031 coast across the River Dee viaduct at Chester with a Pathfinder Tours charter from Chester to West Ruislip. *Mrs J. A. Clough*

Left: Hired by VSOE for charter work, No 50017 was repainted at Crewe South depot into 'Coronation Scot' maroon. The locomotive is seen working empty stock from Westbury to Bath past Freshford before forming the 17.06 to Manchester on 22 July 2000. *John Chalcraft*

Right: **A complete stripdown, rewiring and refurbishment is being undertaken on No 50026 at MoD Bicester on 21 September 1999. External restoration is complete and the power unit (visible on the right) has also received attention.** *Paul Spracklen*

Below: **When the Fifty Fund decided to paint No 50044 into two-tone BR green as D444, Tony Middleton did the job virtually single-handed, with some help from Paul Furtek. The honour of providing the photograph used here goes, fittingly, to the painter. The locomotive is seen at Old Oak Common.** *A. N. Middleton*

9 ___The Portuguese 'Class 50s'___

THE ORDER

EE's DP2 prototype helped to win its builder a further (albeit small) order, which came when Portuguese National Railways (CP), then still a private concern, bought 10 locomotives which, in concept, were more akin to the prototype than the production Class 50 design. A 1965 order from Portugal for 50 machines that were an uprated version of the BR's EE Type 1 (later Class 20), rated at 1,350bhp, were proving successful. When a follow-on order for 17 more locomotives was under discussion, CP enquired about something bigger. At this time a Co-Co wheel arrangement was required for a design of this power and weight. EE was able to point to the Class 50 order placed by BR and demonstrate DP2's track record.

Coincidentally, the British currency was devalued by about 30% at the time, which gave EE a welcome price advantage, and an order for 10 'DP2s' was secured.

At the time of the order, electrification of the railway linking Portugal's two main cities had just been completed. Even so, the maximum speed of any CP diesel or electric did not exceed 120km/h (75mph), and the highest speed ever attained by steam had been around 84mph. The most powerful diesels, rated at 1,600bhp, were of American origin and dated from 1948. This illustrates how big a leap the new design represented, being rated at around 2,600bhp and permitted to run at up to 140km/h (87mph).

Although detailed design work for what would become CP's '1800' class had

Originally painted blue, with white speed whisker, the '1800' class was bought to haul passenger and freight from the main Lisbon–Porto line to the Spanish border. This April 1974 picture is not only a rare illustration of the class during this period but also depicts No 1803 off its normal route at Espinho, just south of Porto, on an engineer's train. It had been through Entroncamento Works two months previously.
R. Bradley

On arrival in the Southern Zone, the '1800s' were assigned to the Directo (now called Inter Regional) services from Barreiro to Vila Real de Santa Antonio. These trains conveyed through coaches for Lagos, detached at Tunes. On 17 March 1988 No 1802 passes Pinherio with the 08.10 to Barreiro.
David N. Clough

already begun, the contract between CP and EE was not signed until 7 June 1968. It is probably fair to say that, conceptually, this was what EE would have preferred to build for BR – the only use of electronics was in the control of main-generator excitation, radiator-fan drive was direct from the engine, and 'old-technology' oil-wetted filters were used for engine-compartment filtration, while a shaft drive was used for the compressor and a belt drive off the main-generator shaft turned the auxiliary generator; contrast these aspects with Class 50 and compare them with DP2.

Most engine and some auxiliary equipment components were interchangeable with CP's other EE diesels, of the '1400' class. The diesel engine was the contemporary 16-cylinder version of the standard EE powerplant, with a site rating of 2,584bhp due to the prevailing ambient temperature.

Whereas BR's Class 50 has four turbochargers, partly to fit better within the constraints of the British loading

gauge, this limitation did not apply in Portugal, which has the standard Continental loading gauge, albeit with a 5ft 6in track gauge. The two large turbochargers give rise to a greater degree of gas excitation than found on Class 50 and result in a more pronounced turbocharger whistle, throwing the exhaust higher into the air. This, together with the lack of noise from the radiator-fan motor (evident with Class 50), explains why the '1800s' are often said to sound more like a BR Class 40 and probably very similar to DP2.

Eleven powerplants, numbered IH7320-30, were supplied, thus providing one spare. (Although the numbers are not even close to the main Class 50 series, by a stroke of fate, when BR ordered two extra engines as spares for the Class 50 pool these were numbered IH7319 and IH7331.) Having a spare engine proved prudent, because over the years two engine blocks were damaged beyond repair and scrapped, leaving just sufficient for the surviving locomotives.

The main generator was essentially identical to that found in Class 50. It had a rating of 1710kW, 1800A, 950V at 850rpm. There was no need to fit a train-heat generator because there was no prospect of coaching stock requiring an electric train supply, carriage-heating being by propane heaters similar to those on the first generation of DMUs built for BR.

Unsurprisingly, the six traction motors fitted were the standard EE538 type. By this time over 3,000 similar motors were in use worldwide, notably on BR Classes 37, 50 and 55. Rated at 270kW each, the '1800' traction motors differed from their Class 37 and 50 equivalents only in having a gear ratio of 66:19, as opposed to 53:18; no doubt this reflected the locomotives' lower anticipated maximum speed of 140km/h (87mph). Three stages of field-weakening gave a very good speed range over which full power was available. Generator-unloading does not occur until a speed of just over 120km/h (75mph) is reached.

Maximum tractive effort was 57,300lb, and the continuous rating 38,800lb at 31km/h (19mph). The performance specification set by CP called for the acceleration of a 200-ton train from rest to 140km/h in 5min and the haulage of an 800-ton freight up a 1.5% (1-in-67) grade at 33km/h. Note how the continuous-rating speed matched very closely the latter performance requirement, this being achieved by careful selection of the traction-motor gear ratio to avoid the risk of overheating the main generator. Sanding gear was fitted for added adhesion and remained in use throughout the life of the class. Another CP requirement was that performance should match that of contemporary electric traction, so that schedules could be maintained when the overhead power was switched off. Operation at altitudes up to 2,950ft had also to be accommodated.

Multiple-working jumper ports were fitted in the centre of the cab front and allowed operation with either a '1400' or another '1800'. The cab instrument cowling was very similar to that of DP2, but an oddity was the ammeter, which measured traction-motor current rather than main generator current. The customary Continental-pattern wheel for the driver's power controller allowed stepless control after the initial shunting notch. The fuel tanks held 1,000 gallons, giving a very useful range. Although built with only vacuum train braking, air-brake equipment was added later. (Another modification would be carried out during

For many years the afternoon 'Sotavento' ('Southern Wind') Rapidos (Inter Cities) crossed at Funcheira. On 20 February 1987 No 1807 arrives with the 15.00 Barreiro–Faro as No 1801 waits to head north with the 15.10 from Faro. *David N. Clough*

the early 1980s, when a bodyside door was cut roughly midway between the cabs to improve access to the engine room.)

Main external dimensions (with Class 50 figures in brackets) are length over buffers 61ft 2in (68ft 6in), width 10ft 8in (9ft 1in) and height 14ft (12ft 9in), which explains why the '1800s' appear tall and broad to British eyes. The overall weight of 110 tons was within the CP's target of 114 tons and ensured availability over the main routes.

Construction of No 1801 at Vulcan Foundry was in the mixed-gauge erecting shop. This was concurrent with the last of the BR Class 50s, and it is surprising that no photographs are known to exist of D449 alongside No 1801, because the former was outshopped in late November 1968, whilst the latter was inspected by CP in early December. Works numbers in the series EE3882-91 were assigned, along with Vulcan Foundry numbers D1246-55.

Livery when new was dark blue for the bodysides, with an aluminium colour for the roof and a grey bodyside stripe extending round the cab fronts; buffer-beams were red and underframe and bogies black, while the tyres were picked out with white rims.

Not long after the class had been delivered there emerged a potential requirement for a further 10 locomotives. Consideration was being given to extracting mineral reserves high in the hills at the eastern end of the Douro Valley. CP envisaged that a further 10 '1800s' would be required to handle this traffic, but nothing came of the project.

EARLY SERVICE

No 1801 arrived in Portugal on 26 December. Initial testing clearly went well, because entry into service followed on 13 January 1969. No 1810 completed the class eight months later, on 14 August.

Initial duties assigned to the class were in the Central Zone and involved two routes. The more important was the Beira Alta line, which leaves the Lisbon–Oporto main line at Pampilhosa and is one of the main international corridors into Spain. The principal service over this steeply graded line was (and is) the 'Sud Express', at that time running daily between Lisbon and Paris. An '1800' took over from a CP electric at Pampilhosa and continued as far as Medina del Campo, deep in Spain.

CP continued to use the sanders fitted to the '1800s' throughout their life. Separated by the sand pile, Nos 1801 and 1804 are depicted at Barreiro depot on 16 March 1988. *David N. Clough*

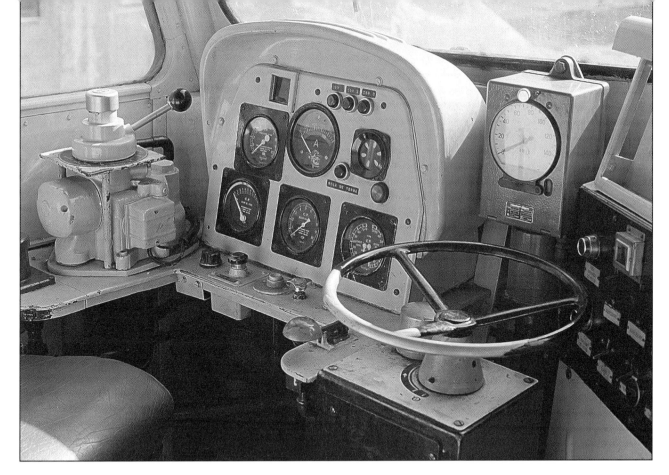

Except for the traditional Continental-pattern 'wheel' form of power controller, the '1800' driver's desk looks more like that of DP2 than a Class 50 (See page 13 by way of comparison).
David N. Clough

Due to the high level of unemployment at home, a significant number of Portuguese went to work in France during the 1960s, and there was a second through service between these countries, dubbed the 'Emigrant Train', and this too was '1800'-powered as far as Medina del Campo. The class also handled all the principal passenger and freight movements over the Beira Alta line. A report from 1972 suggests other services were rostered for the EE '1400s'.

The second route over which the '1800s' were used was the Western line. This runs north from Lisbon, roughly parallel to the coast, and joins the Lisbon–Oporto main line at Alfarelos, roughly halfway between the two cities. Although a secondary passenger route, it carried a significant quantity of freight to the port at Lisbon, where the class also saw action.

Routine maintenance was carried out at a small two-road shed at Pampilhosa, with heavier tasks assigned to the larger facilities at Figueira da Foz, at the northern extremity of the Western line. Portugal's largest railway works at Entroncamento took care of major overhauls, along with those of the '1400' class.

From 1973 CP adopted a revised livery for its main-line diesels fleet. The style adopted for the '1800s' consisted of orange bodysides and brown cab doors, window surrounds, side grilles and roof, with black below the solebar and for the bogies. orange/white diagonal stripes were applied to the cab fronts, extending beneath the side windows. In some cases the roof-mounted headlight/horn cowl was painted white.

TRANSFER SOUTH

By the late 1970s CoRail stock requiring an electric train supply meant that the '1800s' were no longer suitable for international passenger duty. CP thus ordered 13 new locomotives from Canada and from 1979 redeployed the British diesels in the Southern Zone, where, according to CP reports, the final 'l800' arrived in 1983. For some months during 1980 the arrival of the Canadian locomotives had enabled CP to use two '1800s' on engineers' trains on the Lisbon–Oporto main line, before transfer south.

In 1980 responsibility for the overhaul of CP's entire diesel fleet passed to Barreiro Works, and the adjacent depot took charge of periodic maintenance and repairs of the

Above: The other principal passenger service with which the '1800s' had a long association was the 'Comboio Azul' ('Blue Train'). This was a motorail service linking Faro with Porto, the diesel being in charge as far as Entroncamento. On 12 July 1996 No 1808 assembles its train at Faro.
David N. Clough

Right: Heading for Entroncamento for tyre-turning, on 19 March 1988 No 1805 made a very rare sight at the time on a freight over the line linking the Southern and Central zones. Pictured near Muge, the train is the 11.10 Barreiro–Gaia.
David N. Clough

'1800s' following their transfer south. However, no wheel-lathe was available at the complex, so tyre-turning still required visits to Entroncamento.

Despite not being a wealthy railway, CP always took a pride in its motive power. Maintenance standards were traditionally very high, and it was unusual to see a smoky '1800'. (Contrast this to a Class 50!) Each week there was a day-long examination (classified as V4), while more extensive maintenance was based on miles run. Works overhauls were scheduled every 400,000km (250,000 miles), although major component failure could shorten that. A half-life examination (V1), including a full overhaul of the engine's top end, took place every 200,000km (125,000 miles).

On the Southern Zone the class became the premier motive power, consigning older classes to lesser duties. The '1800s' were assigned the through services between Barreiro (a ferry terminal on the opposite bank of the River Tagus from Lisbon) and the Algarve (Portugal's southern coast). At the time there was also a daily through train linking the Algarve

with Oporto, but in later years this became Fridays-only northbound and Sundays-only southbound. On this service an '1800' was provided over the non-electrified section south of the Tagus, the change of traction being effected initially at Setil and later at Entroncamento; during the summer of 1979 No 1805 was staple motive power.

The class's axle loading permitted utilisation on all lines in this zone, save for one branch from Beja. In addition to the principal daytime passenger services there was deployment on the through overnight merchandise service, reflecting the mixed-traffic characteristic of the design. Fill-in turns at both ends of the main line meant that at least one '1800' was diagrammed to assist with the intensive morning and evening commuter trains into and out of Barreiro. On the Algarve coast line the locomotive off the overnight working from Barreiro would cover a local service diagram. The arrival of extra '1800s' at Barreiro by 1980 saw the class displace air-conditioned, First-class Fiat multiple-units of 1953 vintage from the premier 'Sotavento' ('Southern Wind') express between Barreiro and Faro. This service

Normally the author does not like including collision-damaged locomotives, because the sight can be upsetting to some. However, an exception is made for No 1809 – the one most enthusiasts missed because of collision damage sustained in June 1984. On 1 July, seven days after the collision, it is seen at Tunes.
Owen Brison

gave the only daily opportunity for running
at maximum speed, because it used a new
section of railway, built primarily for
freight use, which was the only stretch on
the Southern Zone where speed above
120km/h was sanctioned.

On 23 June 1984 No 1809 suffered
severe collision damage at Loule while
working the 09.55 Faro–Barreiro – a new
train for that summer's timetable.
Approaching Loule, the driver realised the
brakes were inoperative, this being the
first point where a brake application
would have been needed after leaving
Faro. Knowing he was booked to cross an
eastbound local service, he sounded the
horn continuously. Realising there was a
problem, the driver of the other train
stopped outside Loule and instructed his
passengers to alight, thereby preventing
any fatalities. Single-cab locomotive
No 1206 had been travelling bonnet-first
and thus acted as a skewer onto which
No 1809 impaled itself, while the first
coach behind the '1800' bent upwards in
the middle in an alarming way. Although
No 1809 was worked on at Barreiro
Works, this never progressed beyond
producing an intact bodyshell, and this
was eventually scrapped in December
1993. CP decided to cannibalise this

locomotive so its components could keep
the rest of the class in traffic and because
the 10th locomotive could be spared.

CP diagramming required around 80%
availability. Even after No 1809's demise,
seven locomotives were diagrammed for
daily use – a situation which continued
until 1998, when weekend freight
operation reduced this. Indeed, it was not
unusual for all nine class members to be
active simultaneously, but, equally,
unplanned failures and all-too-frequent
collision damage could result in only six
being operative. Nevertheless, CP's
achievements in maintaining high
availability speak well for the
organisation of the railway: it had to
contend with the same problems of spare
parts availability from EE as did BR yet
did not seem to allow this to affect the
serviceability of its fleet.

DOWNGRADING BEGINS

From 1994, when extra air-conditioned
coaches became available for the limited-
stop Barreiro–Faro expresses that
superseded the 'Sotavento', motive power
capable of providing an electric train
supply had to be substituted. Indeed, the
lack of this facility on the '1800s' brought
about the biggest change, from May 1998,

when sectorisation saw them placed in the ownership of the freight sector. Their geographical sphere of utilisation did not change too much, however, and spare locomotives were often borrowed by the passenger sector. Whilst the change was frustrating for enthusiasts wanting to ride behind the class, photographers gained more variety over some freight-only lines in the Southern Zone. In the summer of 1998 Lisbon staged an Expo event, for which CP repainted an example of each class of locomotive and DMU into its former livery, and on 14 May No 1801 emerged from Barreiro in near-original guise.

The beginning of the end came on 24 July 2000, when the freight sector declined to fund works overhauls. No 1801 was the first casualty: taken out of service on 14 July after hauling the Setubal Docks–Azambujal (General Motors) car train, it was assigned to Barreiro Works, but its planned overhaul was cancelled, and its main generator used to replace a defective unit in No 1802. No 1804 was the next to become due an overhaul, its last duty being to substitute for a '1900'-class locomotive on the 1,120-tonne Nerves Corvo–Praias Sado pyrites service on 30 May 2001. On 23 March 2001, meanwhile, having earlier brought empty ammonia tanks into the nearby Quimigal chemical works, No 1806 was running light off Barreiro depot when it was involved in a collision with '1900' No 1909 opposite the freight yard; this was No 1806's second collision in the space of a year (both damaging No 1 end), it having previously had a mishap with No 1931, and, not surprisingly, repairs were not authorised. Components from all three '1800s' were used to keep the remaining six class members in traffic.

In January 2002 the author made an enquiry of CP concerning the run-down schedule, and this elicited the information that all the survivors were to be sidelined at the end of the following month – the first that enthusiasts knew of the decision. A daily average across only four weekday turns of 270km made the '1800s' expensive for the work being done, and a forecast monthly saving of £40,000 was envisaged by squeezing extra utilisation out of other diesel classes. To an extent the '1800s' suffered the same fate as their British cousins, being a small class numerically.

February 2002 saw the surviving '1800s' active on un-diagrammed engineering movements associated with upgrading the Algarve main line, as well as on the usual ammonia tanks from Lavradio to Alverca, cement from Praias Sado to Estremoz, coal from Sines to Loule and salt from Loule to Praias Sado. Whilst obviously not as glamorous as the 'Sud Express', these workings carried important regular flows for CP, with that to Estremoz loading to not far off 1,000 tonnes at times.

The last known workings, on 1 March, involved No 1807 on the Lavradio–Alverca tanks and No 1810 on the Estremoz cement. On the passenger front, No 1807 was hired as emergency cover on 24 February for the daytime diagram on the morning Inter Regional from Barreiro to the Algarve, returning in the afternoon; since 1998 such hiring-in had been fairly common when there was a shortage of '1930'-class traction, but this was almost certainly the last '1800' to appear on a scheduled passenger train.

Not surprisingly, the National Railway Museum at Entroncamento has claimed an '1800' for both exhibition and use on special charters.

IN RETROSPECT

The '1800' class was neither an overwhelming success nor a disaster. British enthusiasts tend to over-regard the performance and draw too favourable a comparison to the BR Class 50s. They performed very competently and were a very useful tool for CP. Drivers liked the comfortable cab, ride and quietness. Unsurprisingly, they were not as strong as the more powerful '1900s' and '1930s'.

Examination of the mileage records for individual locomotives suggests that the initial period of employment on the Central Zone was not quite as intensive as subsequently. Prior to reallocation, the average mileage was 100,000km (62,500 miles); afterwards it was 123,000km (77,000 miles). Taking account of CP route mileage and service intensity, the latter figure demonstrates a very creditable performance. In fact the allocated duties during the mid-1990s had clearly been stepped up, because CP was running more services. Average annual mileages per locomotive were now 137,000km (85,700 miles) and thus similar to an Old Oak Common-based Class 50 after 1987. From 1998, when the '1800s' was taken into freight ownership, rostering was less intense and mileages were reduced in consequence.

During a meeting with the works engineer at Barreiro in 1988, the author gained a good perspective of the current situation. The main problem areas related to main-generator insulation and commutation, turbochargers, bogies and the availability of spares. Leaving the bogies to one side, the other problem areas would have been recognised by British Rail engineers responsible for a Class 50. In February 1988 the class averaged 8,700 miles per casualty. Again, this would have been regarded as typical for Class 50 at the time. In fairness, however, the '1800s' were no more or less problematic than any other class of large diesel found on CP. The main-generator problems were not as severe as on BR, for several reasons: flashovers during the early years brought a decision by CP to derate the engine to 2,400bhp (taking some stress off the main generator), while maintenance appears generally to have been of a higher standard than found on BR; moreover, the class did little work above 75mph, and the track was certainly of a better quality than found on the Waterloo line.

'1800' class individual locomotive details					
CP No	To traffic	Last overhaul	Withdrawn	Reason	Total km from new
1801	13/1/69	6/96	1/10/00	Due overhaul	3,526,582
1802	28/2/69	10/97	1/3/02	Surplus	3,627,106
1803	13/4/69	3/98	1/3/02	Surplus	3,831,143
1804	26/4/69	1/97	26/7/01	Due overhaul	3,661,334
1805	15/5/69	12/99	1/3/02	Surplus	3,498,935
1806	19/6/69	6/99	26/7/01	Collision	3,772,286
1807	10/7/69	7/98	1/3/02	Surplus	3,683,006
1808	25/7/69	12/98	1/3/02	Surplus	3,496,576
1809	3/8/69	1/84	23/6/84	Collision	1,464,000
1810	14/8/69	6/97	1/3/02	Surplus	3,720,653

Appendix

TECHNICAL SPECIFICATION

Diesel engine	EE 16CSVT 16-cylinder four-stroke
Main generator	EE840/4B; continuous rating 1,800A, 970V, 1,746kW @ 850rpm
Train-heating generator	EE915/1B; rating 320kW @ 800V, 550rpm
ETH index	61
Auxiliary generator	EE911/5C; continuous rating 600A, 110V, 66kW @ 450rpm
Traction motors (6)	EE538/5A; continuous rating 600A, 485V, 290kW @ 540rpm, with three stages of field-weakening
Fuel tank capacity	1,055 gallons
Minimum curve radius	4 chains
Maximum axle load	19 tons 10cwt
Route Availability	6
Multiple working	Orange Square (only with Class 50)
Length over buffers	68ft 6in
Overall width	9ft 1¼in
Overall height	12ft 9¹/₁₆in

	Class 50/0	Class 50/1
Engine brake horsepower (bhp)	2,700	2,400
Maximum tractive effort (lb) (at 2,400A main-generator current)	48,000	56,700
Continuous tractive effort (lb) (at 1,800A main-generator current)	33,000 at 23.5mph	41,600 at 16.6mph
Rail horsepower (rhp) at continuous-rating speed	2,070	1,840
Full power range (mph)	15-87	10.5-76
Maximum design speed (mph)	105	80
Maximum service speed (mph)	100	80
Traction-motor gear ratio	53:18	59:16
Weight in working order (tons)	117	114

	50001 Dreadnought	50002 Superb	50003 Temeraire	50004 St. Vincent	50005 Collingwood
Former No	D401	D402	D403	D404	D405
Works No	D1143	D1142	D1144	D1145	D1146
EE Co No	3772	3771	3773	3774	3775
Accepted by BR	06.12.1967	22.12.1967	15.01.1968	22.12.1967	12.01.1968
Renumbered	21.03.1974	23.04.1974	15.02.1974	02.02.1974	26.08.1974
Named	10.04.1978	21.03.1978	09.05.1978	09.05.1978	05.04.1978
Plaque fitted		12.11.1980		09.09.1988	21.11.1987
Refurbished	30.04.1980 (4th)	28.10.1983 (49th)	19.09.1980 (8th)	31.10.1980 (9th)	27.08.1982 (34th)
Depots	CD 12.67 BR 07.73 OC 05.74 LA 04.76	CD 12.67 BR 11.73 OC 05.74 LA 04.76	CD 01.68 BR 03.74 LA 04.74	CD 12.67 BR 01.74 OC 05.74 LA 04.76	CD 01.68 BR 03.74 OC 05.74 LA 04.76
Liveries	A, B, F	A, B, C, E, G	A, B, C, F	A, B	A, B, G
Sectors	NXXA 05.1987 NSSA 30.09.1988 NWXA 20.05.1990	NXXA 05.1987 NSSA 30.09.1988 NWXA 20.05.1990	RXXA 05.1987 NSSA 10.07.1988 NWXA 20.05.1990	PXXA 05.1987 DCWA 09.05.1988	RXXA 05.1987 DCWA 10.07.1988 NSSA 14.05.1989
Classified history	06.08.1971 L ZC 02.04.1974 I ZC 30.04.1980 R ZF 01.08.1984 I ZF 24.01.1988 F LA	05.09.1970 L ZC 04.11.1972 I ZC 15.10.1975 L ZC 22.01.1980 I ZF 28.10.1983 R ZF 07.02.1987 I ZF	24.07.1971 L ZC 05.06.1976 I ZC 19.09.1980 R ZF 06.04.1984 I ZF 09.03.1988 F LA	28.03.1970 L ZC 21.10.1972 I ZC 13.02.1975 L ZC 31.10.1980 R ZF 02.10.1984 I ZF	29.09.1971 L ZC 26.08.1974 I ZC 21.11.1978 I ZF 27.08.1982 R ZF 25.03.1986 I ZF
Condemned	14.00 19.04.1991 LA (33rd)	16.00 09.09.1991 LA (40th)	10.00 15.07.1991 LA (34th)	08.00 22.06.1990 LA (14th)	10.00 11.12.1990 LA (24th)
Reason	Engine	Engine	Main generator	Main generator	Engine
Hours	6,930	8,043	6,898	9,684	9,190
Last passenger	10.04.1991 2V07 0745 Bas-E	22.08.1991 1V11 1100 W-E (f-S)	01.07.1991 IV22 2040W-YJ*-	23.04.1990 1A45 09.18 Ply-Pd (t-E)	15.11.1990 1V09 09.15 W-E
Last working	(as above)	(as above)	(as above)	10.45 ERiv-YJ*	(as above)
Date OOS	10.04.1991	22.08.1991	01.07.1991	26.04.1990	15.11.1990
Disposal	Booth, Rotherham	Devon Diesel Soc, South Devon Railway Totnes	MC, Glasgow	Booth, Rotherham	Coopers, Old Oak
Notes	50001/2 had transposed works numbers – see also 50046/7	See 50001 note			

General explanatory notes on page 160

	50006 Neptune	50007 Hercules (1)	50008 Thunderer	50009 Conqueror	50010 Monarch
Former No	D406	D407	D408	D409	D410
Works No	D1147	D1148	D1149	D1150	D1151
EE Co No	3776	3777	3778	3779	3780
Accepted by BR	23.01.1968	12.03.1968	06.02.1968	06.02.1968	21.02.1968
Renumbered	04.03.1974	12.04.1974	18.02.1974	07.01.1974	07.03.1974
Named	25.09.1979	06.04.1978	01.09.1978	08.05.1978	16.03.1978
Plaque fitted		25.02.1984	20.09.1979		
Refurbished	14.11.1979 (1st)	08.03.1983 (41st)	04.12.1981 (25th)	24.12.1981 (27th)	27.05.1981 (17th)
Depots	CD 03.68 BR 05.74 LA 05.74 CD 05.74 LA 01.76	CD 03.68 LA 05.74	CD 03.68 BR 04.76 LA 05.76	CD 03.68 LA 05.74	CD 02.68 LA 02.76
Liveries	A, B, C	A, B, D	A, B, C, D	A, B, G	A, B, C, D
Sectors	DXXA 05.1987	DXXA 05.1987 DXXD 10.1987 RXXA 30.09.1988 DCWA 08.10.1988 NSSA 14.05.1989 NWXA 20.05 1991	PXXA 05.1987 NXXA 25.05.1988 DCWA 13.08.1988 NWXC 25.01.1991 DCWA 23.06.1991	DXXA 05.1987 NXXA 10.1987 DCWA 09.05.1988 NSSA 14.05.1989 NWXA 20.05.1990 NWXC 14.10.1990	NXXA 05.1987 DCWA 09.05.1988
Classified history	03.03.1970 L ZC 05.06.1973 I ZC 16.09.1976 L ZC 14.11.1979 R ZF 17.02.1984 I ZF	02.07.1971 L ZC 12.04.1974 I ZC 19.07.1979 I ZF 08.03.1983 R ZF 02.04.1987 F LA	12.06.1971 L ZC 09.07.1974 I ZC. 18.01.1978 L ZF 04.12.1981 R ZF 28.02.1986 I ZF	31.10.1970 L ZC 07.01.1974 I ZC 10.06.1977 L ZF 24.12.1981 R ZF 07.11.1985 I ZF	31.10.1970 L ZC 12.09.1973 I ZC 10.08.1977 L ZF 27.05.1981 R ZF 22.04.1985 I ZF
Condemned	14.00 20.07.1987 LA (2nd)	12.00 31.03.1994 LA (50th) (2)	13.50 05.06.1992 LA (46th)	12.00 11.01.1991 LA (27th)	09.00 27.09.1988 LA (8th)
Reason	Main generator	Not required	Not required	Collision	Engine failure
Hours	7,935	9,624	8,537	10,991	6,544
Last passenger	04.06.1987 1V07 0700 W-E	26.03.1994	23.11.1991 1Z37 1420 Nq-MAN	07.12.1990 1V53 0944 Glas-Ply (f-T)	30.07.1988 1V59 1150 Glas-Ply*
Last working	(as above)	26.03.1994 1Z50 1735 Pz-Pd	(as above)	21.12.1990 La-Br hauling 3 DMUs	(as above)
Date OOS	04.06.1987		23.11.1991	03.01.1991	30.07.1988
Disposal	Berry-Leicester	Class 40 Appeal Midland Railway, Butterley	VSOE Crewe C.S	Coopers-Old Oak	Coopers-Laira
Notes		*1* Renamed Sir Edward Elgar and repainted green 25.02.1984 *2 Withdrawn 15.07.1991 Reinstated 20.03.1992*	*Painted in allover blue with no logo 01.91*		* Failed near Bromsgrove Carried a blue roof after a repaint in Laira in 1983

	50011 Centurion	50012 Benbow	50013 Agincourt	50014 Warspite	50015 Valiant
Former No	D411	D412	D413	D414	D415
Works No	D1152	D1153	D1154	D1155	D1156
EE Co No	3781	3782	3783	3784	3785
Accepted by BR	19.03.1968	28.02.1968	06.03.1968	24.04.1968	02.04.1968
Renumbered	07.02.1974	01.02.1974	19.06.1974	11.04.1974	16.03.1974
Named	01.09.1979	03.04.1978	19.04.1978	30.05.1978	21.04.1978
Plaque fitted	15.05.1986				
Refurbished	20.04.1983 (43rd)	06.05.1981(16th)	26.06.1980 (6th)	07.12.1983 (50th)	19.02.1981 (13th)
Depots	CD 03.68 BR 02.74 LA 05.74	CD 03.68 LA 05.76	CD 03.68 LA 05.74	CD 04.68 LA 05.74	CD 04.68 LA 05.74
Liveries	A, B, C	A, B	A, B	A, B, C	A, B, D
Sectors	Withdrawn before sectorisation	PXXA 05.1987 DCWA 09.05.1988	NXXA 05.1987	RXXA 05.1987	DXXA 05.1987 NXXA 10.1987 DCWA 09.05.1988 NXWC 25.01.1991 DCWA 23.06.1991
Classified history	04.07.1970 L ZC 30.12.1972 I ZC 17.03.1975 L ZC 30.05.1980 I ZF 20.04.1983 R ZF	17.07.1970 L ZC 15.01.1973 I ZC 07.12.1975 L ZC 06.05.1981 R ZF 25.03.1985 I ZF	29.09.1970 L ZC 07.02.1973 I ZC 25.11.1975 L ZC 26.06.1980 R ZF 12.09.1984 I ZF	02.09.1970 L ZC 10.03.1973 I ZC 20.03.1976 L ZC 15.03.1980 I ZF 07.12.1983 R ZF	17.01.1970 L ZC 23.09.1972 I ZC 28.05.1975 L ZC 19.02.1981 R ZF 14.11.1984 I ZF
Condemned	10.30 24.02.1987 ZC (1st)	10.00 16.01.1989 LA (9th)	04.00 06.04.1988 OC (4th)	08.00 14.12.1987 LA (3rd)	14.00 05.06.1992 LA (47th)
Reason	Engine testbed	Main generator	Fire damage	Engine to 50149	Not required
Hours	8,234	7,409	7,257	7,621	10,274
Last passenger	12.02.1987 1F11 0752 Twy-Pd	30.11.1988 1V18 1810 W-E	19.03.1988 1F52 19.09 Pd-Ox	08.10.1987 2C27 2151 E-NA	23.11.1991 1Z37 14.20 Nq-MAN
Last working	20.02.1987 3S15 12.10 Pz-Glas parcels from Ply-Crewe	30.11.1988 5V18 2215 E-La ecs*	(as above)	08.10.1987 5C27 2225 NA-La ecs	(as above)
Date OOS	23.02.1987	30.11.1988	21.03.1988	08.10.1987	24.11.1991
Disposal	BREL Crewe 09.1992	Berry, Leicester	Berry, Old Oak	Berry, Leicester	Manchester Class 50 Group, Bury
Notes	Cab at the Railway Age Crew				Painted into 'Dutch' livery 1.91

	50016 Barham	50017 Royal Oak	50018 Resolution	50019 Ramillies	50020 Revenge
Former No	D416	D417	D418	D419	D420
Works No	D1157	D1158	D1159	D1160	D1161
EE Co No	3786	3787	3788	3789	3790
Accepted by BR	24.04.1968	02.04.1968	11.04.1968	23.04.1968	29.04.1968
Renumbered	13.12.1973	16.02.1974	21.03.1974	13.12.1973	17.02.1974
Named	03.04.1978	16.04.1978	06.04.1978	18.04.1978	07.07.1978
Plaque fitted					
Refurbished	18.12.1981 (26th)	09.02.1980 (2nd)	17.12.1982 (40th)	29.03.1980 (3rd)	10.03.1981 (14th)
Depots	CD 04.68 BR 05.74 LA 04.75	CD 04.68 BR 05.74 CD 05.74 LA 01.76	CD 04.68 BR 05.74 LA 05.76	CD 04.68 BR 05.74 LA 07.75	CD 05.68 BR 05.74 LA 05.75
Liveries	A, B, G	A, B, D, E, G	A, B, E, F	A, B, D, E	A, B
Sectors	DXXA 05.1987 NXXA 10.1987 DCWA 09.05.1988 NSSA 14.05.1989 NWXA 20.05.1990	NXXA 05.1987 NSSA 30.09.1988 NWXA 20.05.1990	NXXA 05.1987 NSSA 09.1988 NWXA 20.05.1990	NXXA 05.1987 NSSA 30.09.1988 DSCW 22.02.1989	DXXA 05.1987 FXXL 10.1987 DCWA 09.05.1988
Classified history	22.05.1970 L ZC 04.12.1973 I ZC 26.11.1977 L ZF 18.12.1981 R ZF 22.10.1985 I ZF	12.01.1971 L ZC 24.03.1973 I ZC 09.02.1980 R ZF 13.12.1983 I ZF 15.02.1988 F LA	02.02.1971 L ZC 21.03.1974 I ZC 20.06.1979 I ZF 17.12.1982 R ZF 19.01.1987 F LA	19.09.1970 L ZC 13.12.1973 I ZC 29.03.1980 R ZF 13.04.1984 I ZF	06.06.1970 L ZC 23.12.1972 I ZC 31.12.1975 L ZC 10.03.1981 R ZF 05.09.1984 I ZF
Condemned	10.00 03.08.1990 LA (17th)	16.00 09.09.1991 LA (41st) (2)	10.00 22.07.1991 LA (36th)	13.00 19.09.1990 LA (20th)	14.00 27.07.1990 LA (16th)
Reason	Main generator	Main generator	Engine	Main generator	Engine
Hours	8,592	7,639	10,086	12,444	9,276
Last passenger	19.06.1990 2V05 0557 S-E	04.09.1991 1O29 0530 YJ-W*	16.07.1991 2V05 0615 S-E	13.08.1990 2O04 1737E-W (f-Hon)	05.05.1990 1Z17 1400 Meldon Quarry-Bristol TM
Last working	(as above)	(as above)	(as above)	28.08.1990 1230 Hth-ERiv	15.05.1990 Eriv-Br CE train
Date OOS	19.06.1990	04.09.1991	16.07.1991	28.08.1990	16.05.1990
Disposal	Booth, Rotherham	John Kennedy Tyseley	MC, Glasgow	Cl 50 Loco Assoc, Mid Norfolk Railway	Booth, Rotherham
Notes		*1. Painted Railfreight General triple-grey in 1999 Painted maroon in 2000 2. Withdrawn 22.7.1991 reinstated 23.7.1991*		*Painted into all-over blue (no logo) 7.89*	

	50021 Rodney	50022 Anson	50023 Howe	50024 Vanguard	50025 Invincible
Former No	D421	D422	D423	D424	D425
Works No	D1162	D1163	D1164	D1165	D1166
EE Co No	3791	3792	3793	3794	3795
Accepted by BR	01.05.1968	07.05.1968	08.05.1968	21.05.1968	31.05.1968
Renumbered	23.11.1973	15.02.1974	18.12.1973	08.05.1974	22.01.1974
Named	31.07.1978	20.04.1978	17.05.1978	15.05.1978	06.06.1978
Plaque fitted					07.05.1981
Refurbished	02.04.1982 (29th)	19.12.1980 (12th)	15.08.1980 (7th)	16.11.1982 (38th)	06.08.1982 (33rd)
Depots	CD 05.68 LA 05.75 OC 03.83 LA 06.88	CD 05.68 BR 02.76 LA 05.76 OC 03.83 LA 05.88	CD 05.68 BR 05.74 LA 05.76 OC 03.83 LA 07.90	CD 05.68 BR 05.74 LA 05.76 OC 03.83 LA 07.90	CD 06.68 BR 05.74 LA 12.76 OC 03.83
Liveries	A, B	A, B	A, B, E, G	A, B, C, F, G	A, B, E
Sectors	NXXA 05.1987 PXXA 10.1987 NSSA 21.05.1988 DCWA 13.08.1988	NXXA 05.1987 RXXA 10.1987 FAWC 10.07.1988 DCWA 12.08.1990	NXXA 05.1987 NWRA 30.09.1988 NWXC 12.07.1990 DCWA 12.08.1990	NXXA 05.1987 NWRA 30.09.1988 NWXA 04.07.1990 NWXC 09.07.1990 NWXA 01.08.1990	NXXA 05.1987 NWRA 30.09.1988 NWXA 04.07.1990 NWXC 09.07.1990 NWXA 01.08.1990
Classified history	20.12.1970 L ZC 23.11.1973 I ZC 23.06.1978 L ZF 02.04.1982 R ZF 02.01.1986 I ZF	05.12.1970 L ZC 19.06.1973 I ZC 20.10.1976 L ZC 19.12.1980 R ZF 08.03.1984 I ZF	26.03.1971 L ZC 18.12.1973 I ZC 18.12.1976 L ZC 15.08.1980 R ZF 18.02.1985 I ZF	08.05.1971 L ZC 13.08.1974 I ZC 03.02.1979 I ZF 16.11.1982 R ZF 06.12.1987 F LA	03.04.1971 L ZC 21.12.1974 I ZC 08.09.1979 I ZF 06.08.1982 R ZF 23.02.1987 F LA
Condemned	21.00 17.04.1990 LA (12th)	14.00 20.09.1988 LA (6th)	12.00 15.10.1990 LA (21st)	14.00 01.02.1991 Wb (29th)	11.30 14.08.1989 OC (11th)
Reason	Engine	Engine	Not required	Fire damage	Derailment
Hours	6,814	7,346	9,685	6,010	4,137
Last passenger	24.11.1989 1320 Liv-Ply (f-E)	14.09.1988 1V12 1157 PHbr-Ply (f-E)	30.09.1990 1043 1723 Pgn-W (t-E)	23.01.1991 1V11 1100 W-E*	06.08.1989 1F87 2115 Ox-Pd †
Last working	15.12.1989 1V54 1330 E-La LE	(as above)	14.10.1990 Swn-Br Bdt	(as above)	(as above)
Date OOS	15.12.1989	15.09.1988	15.10.1990	23.01.1991	06.08.1989
Disposal	50021 Loco Assoc, Tyseley	Berry, Leicester	Gareth Griffiths, Barrow Hill	Coopers, Old Oak	Berry, Old Oak
Notes					† Derailed en-route

	50026 Indomitable	50027 Lion	50028 Tiger	50029 Renown	50030 Repulse
Former No	D426	D427	D428	D429	D430
Works No	D1167	D1167	D1169	D1170	D1171
EE Co No	3796	3797	3798	3799	3800
Accepted by BR	12.06.1968	10.06.1968	18.06.1968	21.06.1968	25.06.1968
Renumbered	29.07.1973	08.01.1974	17.02.1974	03.03.1974	18.03.1974
Named	29.03.1978	17.04.1978	10.05.1978	26.10.1978	10.04.1978
Plaque fitted					
Refurbished	08.12.1982 (39th)	01.08.1983 (47th)	22.10.1982 (36th)	08.06.1982 (32nd)	15.09.1983 (48th)
Depots	CD 06.68 LA 05.74 OC 04.82 LA 07.90	CD 06.68 BR 03.74 LA 04.74 OC 04.82 LA 01.84	CD 06.68 LA 05.74 OC 07.79 LA 01.84	CD 06.68 BR 02.76 LA 12.76 OC 06.79 LA 01.84	CD 06.68 BR 05.74 LA 12.76 OC 07.80 LA 05.89
Liveries	A, B, E	A, B, C, F, G	A, B, C, F	A, B, E, F, G	A, B, F
Sectors	NXXA 05.1987 NWRA 30.09.1988 DXXD 09.05.1988 NXXA 21.05.1988 NSSA 30.09.1988 NWXA 20.05.1990	DXXA 05.1987 FXXL 10.1987	PXXA 05.1987 NXXA 10.1987 NSSA 30.09.1988 NWXA 20.05.1990	RXXA 05.1987 NXXA 10.1987 NSSA 30.09.1988 NWXA 20.05.1990	NXXA 05.1987 NWRA 30.09.1988 NSSA 14.05.1989 MWXA 20.05.1990
Classified history	22.02.1972 L ZC 11.10.1974 I ZC 02.06.1979 I ZF 08.12.1982 R ZF 02.10.1986 F LA	03.09.1971 L ZC 08.01.1974 I ZC 12.03.1980 I ZF 01.08.1983 R ZF 28.12.1987 F LA	04.12.1971 L ZC 16.12.1974.1 ZC 20.12.1978 I ZF 22.10.1982 R ZF 02.09.1987 F LA	19.11.1970 L ZC 28.07.1973 I ZC 26.10.1978 I ZF 08.06.1982 R ZF 17.06.1987 F LA	11.12.1971 L ZC 12.11.1974 I ZC 17.09.1980 I ZF 15.09.1983 R ZF 20.11.1987 F LA
Condemned	10.00 11.12.1990 LA (25th)	15.00 23.07.1991 LA (37th)	14.00 01.02.1991 LA (30th)	15.00 23.03.1992 LA (43rd)	16.20 08.04.1992 (45th)
Reason	Engine	Wheelsets	Engine	Engine	Main generator
Hours	8,039	7,116	6,881	8,706	7,684
Last passenger	05.11.1990 1V09 0915 W-E (f-S)	08.07.1991 1V19 1815 W-E	11.01.1991 1V22 2040 W-YJ	02.01.1992 2V17 1655 W-E*	23.02.1992 2V13 1255 W-E*
Last working	(as above)	08.07.1991 5V19 2215 E-La ecs	11.01.1991 5B22 2315 YJ-Elgh-ecs	(as above)	(as above)
Date OOS	05.11.1990	11.07.1991	11.01.1991	07.01.1992	23.02.1992
Disposal	Paul Spracklen MoD Bicester	Mike Fuller, North Yorks Moors Railway	Coopers, Old Oak	Renown/Repulse Restoration Group, Peak Rail	Renown/Repulse Restoration Group, Peak Rail

GENERAL EXPLANATORY NOTES

Plaque	date on which those of the class which carried replica ship's crests (or GWR crests) had them fitted
Refurbished	date returned to traffic after refurbishment
Condemned	date shown on TOPS as withdrawn (R/I – date reinstated)
Reason	reason for withdrawal; usually major component failure
Hours	denotes TOPS hours since last classified repair
Last Passenger	the last passenger working of the locomotive
Last working	the last known working of the locomotive, if different from the last passenger working
Date OOS	date taken out of service, *i.e.* not available for use
Disposal	shows current owner, or by whom and where cut up
	Booth = Booth Roe Ltd
	MC = MC Metals
	Berry = Vic Berry

CLASSIFIED HISTORY

F   'F' exam
L   light overhaul
I   intermediate overhaul
R   general overhaul and refurbishment
LA   Laira
ZC   Crewe Works
ZF   Doncaster Works

SECTOR

DCWA	Departmental WR
DXXA	Departmental
DXXD	Departmental
FAWC	Railfreight Stone – Westbury
FTLL	Railfreight Chemicals – Laira
FXXL	Freight (General)
NSSA	NSE – Solent & Sarum
NWRA	NSE – Thames
NWXA	NSE – Waterloo–Exeter Class 50
NWXC	NSE – Waterloo–Exeter (reserve)
NXXA	NSE
PXXA	Provincial
RXXA	Parcels

LIVERY

A   large-logo
B   grey roof
C   black roof
D   special livery (see relevant footnote)
E   original NSE
F   revised NSE – light blue
G   revised NSE – darker blue

NB: As every Class 50 carried the original all-over Rail blue without variation, this has been excluded from the table.

LAST WORKINGS

Bas	Basingstoke
Bpl	Barnstaple
Br	Bristol
Btn	Brighton
E	Exeter
Elgh	Eastleigh
ERiv	Exeter Riverside
EJ	Exmouth Junction
Glas	Glasgow Central
Glos	Gloucester
Hth	Heathfield
Hon	Honiton
La	Laira (depot or carriage sidings)
Liv	Liverpool
Man	Manchester
NA	Newton Abbot
OOC	Old Oak Common
Ox	Oxford
Pd	Paddington
Pgn	Paignton
PHbr	Portsmouth Harbour
Ply	Plymouth
Pz	Penzance
S	Salisbury
Sca	Scarborough
Swn	Swindon
T	Totnes
Twy	Twyford
W	Waterloo
Wey	Weymouth
Wb	Westbury
Yk	York
YJ	Yeovil Junction
*	failed *en route*
Bdt	brakedown train
Ecs	empty coaching stock
f-	from
LE	light-engine
t-	to

NB: 'Last working' is the last known revenue-earning duty, usually with coaching stock.